THE ROAD TRIP PILGRIM'S GUIDE

The Road Trip Pilgrim's Guide

WITCHDOCTORS, MAGIC TOKENS,
CAMPING ON GOLF COURSES, AND
EVERYTHING ELSE YOU NEED TO
KNOW TO GO ON A PILGRIMAGE

Dan Austin

SKIPSTONE

Published by Skipstone, an imprint of The Mountaineers Books
Printed in Canada

First printing 2007
10 09 08 07   5 4 3 2 1

Copy Editor: Liz McGehee
Design: Mayumi Thompson
All photographs by author unless otherwise noted.
Cover photograph: © Stefan Schuetz/zefa/Corbis
Frontispiece: *Cape Wrath, Scotland*

ISBN 13: 978-1-59485-081-3

This book is not intended as a substitute for your own judgment; basic rules and regulations should
be considered in any park, city, county, state, or country through which you travel. This book should
be used as an inspirational guide only. The author and publisher disclaim any responsibility for
adverse effects resulting directly or indirectly from information contained herein.

Library of Congress Cataloging-in-Publication Data
Austin, Dan, 1973-
  The road trip pilgrim's guide : witchdoctors, magic tokens, camping on
golf courses, and everything else you need to know to go on a pilgrimage
/ by Dan Austin.
     p. cm.
  ISBN 978-1-59485-081-3
 1. Pilgrims and pilgrimages. I. Title.

BL619.P5A97 2007
203'.51—dc22

                             2007022343

Skipstone books may be purchased for corporate, educational, or other
promotional sales. For special discounts and information, contact our Sales
Department at 1-800-553-4453 or mbooks@mountaineersbooks.org.

Skipstone
1001 SW Klickitat Way
Suite 201
Seattle, Washington 98134
206.223.6303
www.skipstonepress.org
www.mountaineersbooks.org

LIVE LIFE. MAKE RIPPLES.

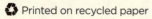 Printed on recycled paper

Contents

Prologue

A PILGRIM'S PARABLE, PART I: MEXICO

It's a dark night in Mexico.

I'm on my mountain bike riding through the deep blackness along the hot, tired Gulf Coast where long fields run down to the ocean. It's late at night and the end of the millennium, December 1999. The traffic on the highway has died down to cicada song and it's time to find a place to camp.

Toward the ocean is the glow of a town. It isn't the warm glow of a New Hampshire village; it's dim, it's tired, it's asthmatic light, but it's something.

I turn down a mangled dirt road bordered on each side by six-foot cement ditches. One little slip of the pedals and that's where I end up.

The ground is so dark that it's hard to distinguish road from sky. And it's so chewed up it feels like somebody took a steam shovel to it. I don't know how anybody navigates it during the day, let alone on this blackest night in all Mexico.

The village gets closer; it looks like the set of a horror film, all the lights pale and dim. My bike gloves are drenched with sweat from gripping the handlebars in a desperate attempt to keep from flying off the road. Without these gloves, my hands would be in shreds.

The road widens and I roll into town.

All I see are vacant houses and empty streets. There's a hot, gaunt breeze blowing off the Gulf, like the soul of the town still lingering, long after the village itself had died. I reach the town center and a run-down plaza. Usually it's tough to camp in villages in Latin America because the kids keep you up half the night asking questions. But there aren't any kids here; there isn't *anyone* here.

I drop my bike, take off my gloves, and toss out the sleeping bag. Then I notice something strange: fireflies.

Fireflies? Here? In Mexico? One by one they appear in the gloom and suddenly I realize they aren't fireflies; they're the burning ends of cigarettes, hanging from the mouths of twenty or so teenagers.

"Planning to camp here?" their leader asks. He's cool and distant and blows his smoke out slow, letting it hang in the air, examining it, like a seer studying runes.

"Maybe," I say, trying to sound nonchalant.

They walk over to my bike. *"Cuesta mucho?"* Expensive?

"Not really," I say. I'd paid twelve hundred dollars for it two weeks before.

He notices my camcorder sitting on the front pouch. "Expensive?" he asks.

"Not really," I say. His friends surround me.

"What are you doing here?" he asks. The smile fades from his face. "No Americans come here."

"I'm biking down to the Yucatán," I say, picking up my bike and sleeping bag. "I'm heading for Chichén Itzá, for the Great Ball Court."

"Long way," he says. "Anybody try to rob you yet?"

"No," I reply.

"That's good," he says. "Gotta be careful."

There's a minisuper (a one-man grocery stand) on the other side of the park. I wheel my bike over as casually as possible. The teenagers come with me, asking lots of questions, all involving how much things cost.

As I approach the stand, the man inside looks up. There are bags under his eyes and gouges across his face that look like knife wounds, but they're just wrinkles. His face is yellow under the gangrene glow of the bulb. A couple near-dead flies buzz around.

"What are you doing here?" he asks, stunned.

"I'm riding down the Gulf Coast," I tell him.

"Americans don't come here," he says, his eyes as large as the yellow bulb, with spots on the pupils like the near-dead flies. "People disappear here all the time. People get killed here."

I try to seem unconcerned. "Oh . . . seems like a nice place . . ."

"You shouldn't be here," warns the man.

The teenagers surround me.

I thank him; I thank the teenagers. I buy a Coke and ask them what they want for Christmas. "Maybe a new bike," they say.

Well, lovely. I hop on my bike. The teenagers move apart and let me pass. I don't look back, but I listen, and soon, to my relief, it's quiet; they're not following me.

I ride as fast as I dare back through town. No wonder no one's around; this place is right out of a Stephen King novel. A wall of darkness moves toward me, the last streetlight disappears behind me, and suddenly I'm immersed in the night again, on that ragged umbilical road between village and highway.

I ride twice as fast as I did getting down here, my handlebars shaking, the bike bouncing all over the place. In the far distance a light passes on the highway. That's where I'm going. It's a long way from here.

I look back to make sure I'm not being followed, and I see two kids on a dirt bike sail through the last streetlight.

Out here in this no-man's-land between the town and the highway, I'm dead meat. No one to help, no one to hear. No wonder they let me go! This is the place to do it!

My heart ramps up. I stand on the pedals. I gotta outrun them to the highway! But when I glance back, they're gaining on me!

Faster . . . I hit a hole and it throws me inches from the cement ditch. I'm all over the road, out of control, careening through the blackness.

I look back. They're still gaining! There's a big kid pedaling and a little kid sitting on the handlebars!

I ride wildly through the chasms of the road, across a stone bridge, and the kids are still gaining! Impossible! They're only fifty feet back and now they're yelling!

"Hey you! You!" Thirty feet! I can't go any faster. It's a miracle I haven't wrecked. I can hear them gulping breath, I'm gulping breath. Twenty feet!

I give it one last push but the kids are still faster, yelling. Ten feet! And I'm only halfway to the highway! There's no way I can outrun them, and I'm in the middle of the emptiness. If I stop fast, I can probably overpower them, unless they have a gun . . .

I hit the brakes. They pull up beside me.

And the little kid on the handlebars hands me my glove.

"You dropped it back in town," he says. And they turn around and ride away.

Introduction

So you want to go on a pilgrimage . . .

Wonderful. You will never regret it. Wanting to go is the first step.

So what is a pilgrimage? Well, the way I've come to understand it, you can take a trip or you can take a pilgrimage. You can escape

from life or escape *to* it. You must always return from a vacation, but you never return from a pilgrimage quite the same. Plus, a pilgrimage is much more fun.

I'm a filmmaker, an author, and an entrepreneur; I've been a New York City bike messenger and a television-show host. Yet, beyond all these things I'm a seeker. A pilgrim. The road has always called to me, but not with the promise of escape; it calls instead with the promise of rebirth. This is the essence of a pilgrimage: returning as a different person than the one who left.

And having a blast in the process, of course.

So, now that you understand that there is a fundamental difference between a vacation and a pilgrimage, between the mind-set of the tourist and that of the seeker, you might wonder, where does one make a pilgrimage to?

Anywhere, really.

Throughout this book, as I talk about what may enhance or guide your pilgrimage, I'll reference a few of my own. There was the mountain-bike ride across America to the Basketball Hall of Fame. There was a six-week trek down the Gulf Coast of Mexico at Christmastime to the Great Ball Court of Chichén Itzá. There was an eight-hundred-mile pilgrimage to a Spokane pub. There was a weekend-long quest to Napa Valley to see about a girl, and there was a two-thousand-mile bike tour of Ireland and Scotland to the hometown of a king . . .

Wait a second. A pilgrimage to a pub? A jock shrine? A ball court? Are these really pilgrimages?

Sure they are.

Though historically religious in nature, pilgrimages do not need to be holy quests. At its heart, a pilgrimage is a journey of importance, to the pilgrim and maybe no one else. Road trip spirituality is as unique as the person who seeks it, often having little to do with any prescribed path. After all, most religions were started by vagabonds, mavericks, and idealistic visionaries with no great love for bureaucracy.

Your pilgrimage could involve fasting, penitence, and self-flagellation. But it could—should—also involve falling in love, dancing all night long, sleeping on the beach, reading Jacques Prévert, biking through torrential rain, crying your eyes out at something so beautiful (or so tragic), crashing with locals, breaking laws, sleeping in hammocks, guzzling Guinness, hitting midnight Mass on Christmas Eve, sleeping in banana fields, making out on top of Mayan temples, indulging in a Japanese onsen, and ultimately, finding that grail of happiness and meaning: **truth to self.**

And this is the essence of being a **road trip pilgrim**.

During the course of my pilgrimages, many friends have joined me, and so they appear throughout this book. My brother Jared has been with me on most of my journeys. You'll like Jared. He's funny, sardonic, brutally honest, and lacks diplomacy with women. He's now a pediatrician.

Among the cast of other characters is Clint, a high school pal of nineteen years (Clint and Jared and I rode across America together); my other brother, Micah, the hitchhiking king; my sister, Alicia, an intrepid Peace Corps volunteer; my friend Alexia (perhaps the world's foremost expert on baths); and many other souls who I took with me or met along the way. A pilgrimage is blessed with a transcendent camaraderie, where years later you and your fellow pilgrims still laugh about getting kicked out of that pub in Ireland. You feel a bond for the rest of your lives. Indeed, sharing the unfolding narrative of your journey together elicits the greatest joys and most powerful personal transformations.

The path and the shrine may be the body of the pilgrimage, but human interaction is the soul.

Just as I can't tell you where to make your pilgrimage and whether to go alone or with others, I can't tell you what your pilgrimage should entail; it's unique to you. I can share with you a little of what I have learned, though, and hopefully provide you with a few ideas that will spark your imagination. No matter what you take from all of this, just promise that you'll do one thing for me.

Promise me that you'll go.

Dan Austin

Brooklyn, New York
June 1, 2007

CHAPTER 1

Before the Journey

CHOOSE A HIGHWAY

"When I was sixteen, all I needed was a two-lane highway. My squirrelly algebra teacher was in the middle of a lecture when I walked out of class and headed for the highway that ran past the school. When I reached the asphalt, a wispy thought came to me, carrying just enough suggestion to guide my hand out with my thumb in the air. A moment later, I was breathing the dusty, sweet smell of alfalfa and manure in the back of a pickup truck. I liked how I felt in the back of that truck, and so when my driver stopped, I thanked him and raised my thumb for another ride to anywhere. I was soon hitchhiking north up Highway 89, hopping from car to pickup and from pickup to minivan. This initial unplanned journey, this spontaneous leap, with only textbooks in my backpack, portended many such adventures to come.

"Curiosity and desire enticed me back to the highway many times. As I walked and hitched, rode and talked, an unfamiliar clairvoyance settled in, casting everything I saw and everyone I met as kindred spirits. An entire population of genuinely kind-hearted people traveled the highways, waiting to help, if only for a few miles. My own place became clearer in the world as I chatted with truckers from Chattanooga, listened to traveling salesmen from Tennessee, entertained a bevy of young vamps from Soda Springs, and discussed poetry with a freelance photographer in Yellowstone. I kept in touch with many of them for years and was even invited to two weddings. When Glen, a sixty-five-year-old publisher from Santa Fe, announced his engagement to Peggy, he thanked me for my advice: 'No man, at any age, is too old to take a chance on love.'

"I didn't need to hitchhike; I had an old Chevy that sailed the freeways like a yacht. But I must have felt there was some-thing for me out there on Highway 89, or else I wouldn't have taken that first ride. Something called to all my senses and kept me on the roads until my entire being was satiated. I think ev-erybody has their own heroic journey, a kind of coming-of-age quest; mine was as a transient in humanity's automobiles.

"No longer a hobo of the highway, I now study literature for the same reasons I hitchhiked. I still search for the human spirit that never hides from clairvoyance and always rewards with inner peace. And, of course, I always pick up hitchhikers."

— *Micah Austin, English grad student,*
Bloomington, Indiana

Some go by land,
Some go by sea,
Some with a map,
Some in mystery . . .
Some go by mind,
Some go by soul,
Some go with god,
Some, never go . . .

— From Pilgrim Go! *(a terrific song written by
folk artist Cherie Call for my Mexico
pilgrimage/film)*

WHAT IS A PILGRIMAGE?

People have been going on pilgrimages for a long time. The pilgrimage is one of our oldest shared cultural traditions. So where do people go?

Some people go to places like Machu Picchu in Peru, sacred city of

the Inca and one of the most visited ancient sites in the world. Hundreds of thousands make a pilgrimage here every year:

some seeking enlightenment,
some seeking adventure;
some for the ancient culture,
some for the miniature llamas.

Very rare, by the way, the miniature llamas.

Other people choose a place like Wantage, England.

King Alfred, who ruled the southern Anglo-Saxon kingdom of Wessex from 871–899, was one of England's (and history's) greatest kings, famously repelling the Vikings who had run roughshod over the rest of Europe for nearly a century.

As his great-many-times-over grandsons—my brothers, Jared and Micah, and I made Wantage the destination for our 2,000-mile mountain

This statue of King Alfred the Great stands in his hometown of Wantage, England.

This is Jack and Dan's Tavern in Spokane, Washington. We made a two-week mountain bike pilgrimage here through the wilds of Idaho.

bike pilgrimage through Europe. Unlike Machu Picchu, we were probably the only pilgrims in Wantage that day, but it is every bit as sacred to us as the ancient Incan city is to others.

Or you may even go to a place like Jack and Dan's Tavern.

Jack Stockton runs the bar. He's the father of John Stockton, legendary point guard for Gonzaga University and then the Utah Jazz. As Utah natives, we'd grown up watching John take apart the competition and had long wanted to make a pilgrimage to this "last outpost" of true Jazz fandom, where locals "dance on the tables," when John hits a parking-lot trey. Like Wantage, this wasn't exactly a Mecca for many either, but it was fun for us, and that's what counts.

So, your journey may lead you to a place sacred to many, a place sacred to a few, or a shrine sacred to virtually no one.

The only thing that matters is that it matters to you.

CHOOSING THE SHRINE

Throughout history, pilgrims have capped their pilgrimages with a diversity of shrines. Destinations like holy mountains and sacred springs have probably been around for as long as people have taken journeys. Human-made shrines, from the megalithic stones of Carnac in France to the magnificent tombs of Egypt, have existed in some form or another for nearly as long. Choose the destination for your pilgrimage well; the shrine will be the magnet pulling you onward through the rigors of the quest.

To give you some ideas for choosing a shrine, I've listed below a few possibilities. The first list is composed of well-known pilgrim destinations, like holy mountains (Mount Fuji) and pop cultural shrines (The Field of Dreams). Many of these places have been visited by pilgrims for centuries. They make fantastic destinations for a pilgrimage and it's fun to tap into the communal energy of thousands of others making the same trek. The second list is composed of shrines that aren't so famous, but may give you some inspiration in choosing a shrine that makes sense to you.

So, your pilgrimage can lead to a place like Machu Picchu, which is already held sacred or revered by millions, or it may lead to a fantastic surfing beach in Australia that's on virtually no one's pilgrim radar save for a few diehards in the know. Each of these shrines, well-known or very personal, is equal as long as the one you choose matters to you.

ESTABLISHED PILGRIMAGE DESTINATIONS

First, here are some of the places visited by pilgrims all the time.

TEMPLE SHRINES

Varanasi, India. Sacred Hindu city on the holy Ganges River.

Chartres, France. Epic gothic cathedral built on a hill once crowned by a grove of trees sacred to druids.

Angkor Wat, Cambodia. Ancient and enormous temple city featuring many of the largest and most spectacular religious buildings in the world.

Angkor Wat, Cambodia

HEALING SHRINES

Caacupé, Paraguay. Thousands trek to Caacupé's famous Basílica de Nuestra Señora de los Milagros in December hoping to be cured.

Cartago, Costa Rica. The city's Basílica de Nuestra Señora de los Ángeles is the destination of many a pilgrim. Touch the sacred stone . . .

Lourdes, France. The Sanctuary of Our Lady of Lourdes is the site of a famous visitation of the Virgin Mary and the most visited healing shrine in the world.

SACRED MOUNTAINS

Croagh Patrick, Ireland. Thousands climb to the top on the last Sunday in July; thousands more climb it throughout the rest of the year.

Mount Fuji, Japan. In the Shinto tradition the mountain is a living being.

Bear Butte, South Dakota. Sacred site of vision quests and pilgrimages for the Lakota Sioux and Cheyenne tribes.

Pilgrims climb to the top of Croagh Patrick near Westport, Ireland.

NATURAL TEMPLES

Iguazú Falls, Brazil/Argentina. On the border of these two countries, this epic waterfall awes millions every year.

Thingvellir, Iceland. Rocky gorge, site of the world's first parliament in AD 930, and meeting place of medieval Icelanders.

Uluru, Australia. Also known as Ayers Rock, this megalithic natural monument is a sacred center of the Dreamtime to the Aboriginal people.

Falls on the Oaxaca River near Thingvellir

HOLY WELLS AND SPRINGS

Chalice Well, Glastonbury, England. Holy well. Its waters, linked to both pagan and early Christian mythology and believed to have great

A holy well in Iceland

healing properties, have never failed to spring forth in more than two thousand years of continual use.

Grey Cliff Spring, Blacksmith Fork Canyon, Utah. Sip the healing waters as they gush from the mountainside.

Tobernault Holy Well, County Sligo, Ireland. One of hundreds of Irish holy wells. The Irish have been taking pilgrimages to holy wells and springs for millennia.

HOT SPRINGS

Pamukkale, Turkey. A gigantic mountain of a hot spring, renowned since the second century BC for its healing waters and visited for centuries by pilgrims; now a major tourist attraction and UNESCO world heritage site.

Talknafjurdur Geothermal Spring, Talknafjurdur, Iceland. A hot spring sacred to the fishermen and women of Talknafjurder, a remote fishing village in the west fjords of Iceland. Fisherfolk from Talknafjurdur and the surrounding villages take pico-pilgrimages up to the spring for a quick dip almost every evening.

Tirthapuri Hot Springs, Tibet. Pilgrims to Mount Kailash often bathe in these sacred waters after their circuit, or *kora,* of the mountain.

SACRED LAKES

Boeng Yeak Lom Crater Lake, Cambodia. Sacred lake to the indigenous people of the Rôtônôkiri province in Cambodia. Legend has it that the lake is home to all sorts of mythical creatures.

Lake Manasarovar, Tibet. Sacred lake near Mount Kailash. Pilgrims walk around the lake, a journey that takes four or five days. Pilgrims to Mount Kailash also sometimes bathe in the chilly waters after their circuit of the mountain.

Loch Ness, Scotland. Pilgrimage destination for millions of monster hunters hoping for a glimpse of the famous "Nessie."

JOURNEY AS SHRINE

Route 66. America's one-time "main street" starts in Chicago and ends in Los Angeles.

Northern Forest Canoe Trail, New York, Vermont, New Hampshire, Maine, and Québec. This water trail follows 740 miles of interconnecting rivers and lakes used for millennia by American Indians. It was recently mapped and completed with portages and primitive campsites, a neat example of a brand-new pilgrimage rising in the paddle ripples of an ancient path.

Trans-Siberian Railroad. Winds 5,772 miles from Moscow to Vladivostok, Russia. One of the world's great rail journeys, the Trans-Siberian hosts road trip pilgrims from all over the world.

POP-CULTURE SHRINES

Graceland, Memphis, Tennessee. The masses converge in droves to pay homage to the King.

The Field of Dreams, Dyersville, Iowa. The original baseball field portrayed in the film *The Field of Dreams* hosts thousands of road trip pilgrims every year.

The Las Vegas Strip, Las Vegas, Nevada. Millions visit from all over the world to lose themselves in the four-mile, amped-up neon wonderland of flashy, facade-driven casinos.

PERSONAL SHRINES

Wantage, England. Hometown of my ancestor, King Alfred the Great.

Arlington Cemetery, Arlington, Virginia. Center of communal and personal sacredness to millions.

The Hero's Mountain, Hyrum, Utah. This 8,400-foot mountain in my hometown backyard is sacred to my family.

The list below consists of places you may not initially consider shrines, like the Guinness Brewery in Dublin. In fact, you may be the only pilgrim to show up, but that personal connection to the shrine is what matters. When choosing a shrine, consider:

If you love to surf . . .

Make a pilgrimage to Big Sur, or ride across France to Biarritz, a celebrated European surf town. Or better yet, make a pilgrimage to that legendary beach *you've* always dreamed about surfing.

The elation at reaching the top of the Hero's Mountain!

If you love Shakespeare...

Stratford-upon-Avon, the Bard's hometown, makes a terrific shrine. Watch a play, enjoy the farmer's market, and camp out. In fact, a nice farmer at the farmer's market in Stratford-upon-Avon gave us more peas than we could eat, all for just a pound sterling. Why? Another pilgrim principle: **When you're on a pilgrimage, almost everyone will want to encourage the quest.**

If you love aviation...

Make a pilgrimage to Kitty Hawk, North Carolina. Hit all the cool, small-town airports along the way.

If you love football . . .

Make a pilgrimage to Canton, Ohio, the Pro Football Hall of Fame.

If you're a firefighter . . .

Stay at fire stations along the way. My friend Anthony did this and got a hero's welcome all across America.

If you love flamenco music . . .

Make a pilgrimage to Seville, Spain, the wellspring of flamenco. Take in all the great local bands as you amble through Andalusia.

If you love literature . . .

Make a pilgrimage to the crib of your favorite author. You could start in Key West, Hemingway's stomping grounds, and end up at his grave in Ketchum, Idaho. Or maybe just run up to Bangor and harass Stephen King.

If you love Coca-Cola . . .

Visit their headquarters in Atlanta, Georgia. You'll be greeted as a saint and given all the Coke you can drink; I guarantee it.

If you seek guidance . . .

Make a pilgrimage to the sites of ancient oracles, like Delphi in Greece or Didyma in Turkey.

If you love Guinness . . .

Make a pilgrimage to the legendary brewery in Dublin, Ireland.

If you love champagne . . .

Make a pilgrimage to the Champagne region of France where authentic champagne is made.

If you're into fossil fuels . . .

Hike the 800-mile Alaska Pipeline from the Gulf of Alaska to the Arctic Ocean and marvel at this wonder of engineering.

If you're not into fossil fuels . . .

Hike the 800-mile Alaska Pipeline as a statement for green energy.

If you feel a kinship with caribou . . .

Make like Karsten Heuer and *migrate* with Canadian caribou herds to their winter retreat.

If you're a basketball junkie . . .

Make a highly recommended pilgrimage to the Basketball Hall of Fame in Springfield, Massachusetts.

If you want to commune with a goddess . . .

Make a pilgrimage to Petra tou Romiou (Aphrodite's Rock) on the island of Cyprus, where Aphrodite, the goddess of love, emerged from the sea.

If you don't know where to go . . .

The ocean is always a powerful shrine. Go until you can go no more.

The possibilities are limitless.

What are you passionate about? What do you love? A pilgrimage connects passion with place via journey.

The eternal allure of the open road

GOOD KARMA PILGRIMAGES

Instead of an established or personal shrine, you may opt for what I call a good karma pilgrimage. This is the sort of journey where the goal is helping people. If there is a physical "shrine," it may be an orphanage, a village, a hospital, or even someone's home. Here are a few examples of good-karma pilgrimages:

88bikes pilgrimage, Phnom Penh, Cambodia. My brother Jared, our friend Nick, and I raised money from individual sponsors to buy bikes for eighty-eight kids at the Palm Tree Center, an orphanage, learning center, and clinic in Phnom Penh, Cambodia. Then Jared and I ran over to Cambodia to buy and distribute the bikes to the children. During the first few weeks of the trip, we explored temples and climbed holy mountains, but the journey's true holy site was the orphanage, our last stop on the pilgrimage and as worthy a shrine as any I have ever visited.

Three happy kids get their first ride!

I will never forget the cry of joy that rang out from all eighty-eight kids when that massive truck loaded full of brand-new bikes backed into the courtyard of the orphanage. Jared and I were mobbed by ecstatic children, hugging us, thanking us, and then bounding around with unbridled happiness. The next day the orphanage staff told us that that morning they were awakened by a symphony of little bike bells as the kids, many of whom had gone to bed with their bikes, had begun riding them around the orphanage at 5:00 AM!

Imagine never really owning anything in your life; then one day, you get a bike, that ultimate symbol of freedom and fun. We raised enough money not only to outfit the kids with new bikes, locks, and helmets, but also to establish bike-repair apprenticeships for some of the older kids and to get a bike shop going at the orphanage where the kids can learn the craft and maybe even make a few bucks on the side. This good karma pilgrimage was as uplifting a journey as any I have ever completed.

Jared, Nick, and I do the 88bikes project every year, choosing a new country and a new orphanage *(www.88bikes.com)*.

A few other examples of good karma pilgrimages:

Three Cups of Tea pilgrimage. Greg Mortenson's good-karma pilgrimage to build schools in rural Pakistan and Afghanistan. You can read about it in his book, *Three Cups of Tea: One Man's Mission to Promote Peace . . . One School at a Time.*

Nepalese libraries. John Wood's good-karma pilgrimage to buy books for Nepalese children, establish libraries and schools, and fund children's educations. You can read about his adventures in his book, *Leaving Microsoft to Change the World: An Entrepreneur's Odyssey to Educate the World's Children.*

A good-karma pilgrimage can lead you anywhere, from the inner city of Chicago to a village in Sri Lanka. One key element is seeing the people you're helping as heroes instead of victims. These courageous souls are striving under often very extreme circumstances. They'll appreciate any help you can give them, but remember they're already making heroic strides on their own.

HOW FAR AND HOW HARD

A pilgrimage can be long or short, arduous or relaxing. It can take a week, a month, or a lifetime. It may lead through deserts, mountains, rain forests, or it may lead from one end of town to the other. Along the way you may encounter mythological monsters, tyrannical camp hosts, beguiling Circes, and many kindhearted souls.

The duration and difficulty of the journey has nothing to do with the importance of the quest.

To compare one pilgrimage to another is antiheroic. However, you might want to think about what length of time or arduousness of journey you are up for. The following examples represent some of the varying degrees of commitment a given pilgrimage might require.

PICO-PILGRIMAGES

Commitment: An afternoon or a few days. Almost everyone can carve out a couple days for a pico-pilgrimage. And don't underestimate the power of a short journey. You can return transformed after just an afternoon or a weekend. Here are a couple examples of possible pico-pilgrimages:

THE ASCENT OF CROAGH PATRICK, IRELAND.

Jared and Micah wave on the summit of Croagh Patrick.

Distance: 2,500 feet of elevation gain and a couple miles of trail
Duration: one to three hours to the top

St. Patrick fasted on top for forty days and nights (or so goes the legend), but you can be up and down in half a day, and man what a view! Like many sacred pilgrimage destinations, the mountain was holy long before Patrick arrived on the scene. For the ancient Celts, it was home to their god Crom Dubh and the primary site of the Lughnasadh harvest festival, during which time only women were allowed to make the ascent, as it was believed to enhance fertility. (Contrast this refreshing tradition with Mount Athos in Greece where men are still the only folks allowed on the mountain.)

THE SPIRAL JETTY, THE GREAT SALT LAKE, NORTHERN UTAH

Distance: 15 miles from the Golden Spike Visitor's Center in northern Utah
Duration: a day-trip by mountain bike or a half-day round-trip by Jeep

One of the most famous works of land art in the world, the spiral jetty rises from the shallow waters of the Great Salt Lake from a remote shore in northern Utah. Constructed by Robert Smithson in 1970, the bumpy ride through stark desert landscape helps you really appreciate your shrine, and yet you can easily do this pico-pilgrimage in half

© *Photo by Micah Austin*

a day. More and more pilgrims visit the Spiral Jetty every year, but it's still pretty remote and serene. Start driving long before dawn and have breakfast as the sun rises.

CRUISING US HIGHWAY 101, WEST COAST OF THE UNITED STATES

Distance: just over 1,500 miles, from Olympia, Washington, to Los Angeles, California

Duration: a leisurely week to ten days of driving

This has become one of the world's most popular journey-as-shrine destinations for road trip pilgrims. For good reason, too: US 101 offers magnificent ocean vistas, beaches, redwood forests, and an abundance of fun and famous towns, such as Big Sur and Lincoln City. Jack Kerouac and his gang explored parts of the route, and tens of thousands more explore it every year. Try biking the 1,500 miles (three to six weeks) for a tremendous middle-path pilgrimage.

> *"Then me and my boys were going to cruise around town, out to the lake if we felt like it, or pedal all the way uphill to the highest point in our part of Milwaukee, near the water reservoir, and look out beyond, feeling like kings of the world. And then, living large, we were going to plunge down Snake Hill, the biggest rush of our lives, taking our feet off the pedals so we could go even faster, pushing the limits of danger and excitement and just letting it rip."*
> — Chris Gardner, from his memoir,
> The Pursuit of Happyness *(Amistad, 2006)*

THE MIDDLE PATH

Commitment: Several weeks to a couple months, more than enough time to get out there and really lose yourself to the road. Here are a couple examples of midrange pilgrimages you probably won't have to sell your house and quit your job to undertake; however, they'll still require internal fortitude, patience, planning, and guts.

THE CIRCUMAMBULATION OF MOUNT KAILASH, TIBET

Distance: 32 miles around the base of the mountain, plus however long it takes you to get there

Duration: three to four weeks of total travel

Though visitation to Mount Kailash is increasing, getting there is still quite an adventure. Sacred to four faiths and billions of people, Mount Kailash is as isolated as it is revered. You may drive, trek, or mountain bike for days or weeks before arriving at the base of the magnificent, solitary, 23,000-foot peak. And then comes the thirty-two-mile hike. The circuit, or *kora,* around Kailash may take weeks if you do it with prostrations, or one to three days if you walk it straight.

WALKING EL CAMINO DE SANTIAGO (PILGRIM'S PATH TO SANTIAGO DE COMPOSTELA, FRANCE/SPAIN)

Distance: nearly 500 miles

Duration: one to two months of solid walking

Buddhists, atheists, surfers, Sikhs, mystics, hedonists, wine bibbers, orthodox Catholics, idealists, anarchists, hermits, poets—you meet just about every sort on the road to Santiago.

One of the most famous pilgrimage routes in the world, the road winds nearly five hundred miles to Santiago de Compostela, where the remains of St. James are believed to rest. For medieval pilgrims who completed the quest, all sins were forgiven. (Not a bad deal, eh?) What's really interesting about this pilgrimage is that most of the people who do it nowadays aren't even devout Christians. They're just road trip pilgrims of every stripe, tapping into an age-old tradition and making it their own. It makes sense; before el Camino was walked by Christians, it was a sacred path for ancient pagans.

TREKKING THE ANCIENT NAKAHEJI PILGRIMAGE ROUTE, KII PENINSULA, JAPAN

Distance: approximately 700 miles

Duration: one to two months of trekking or three to four weeks of biking

One of several pilgrim paths in Japan, this route takes you along the coast of the Kii Peninsula in the footsteps of more than a thousand years of pilgrims. Trekkers bathe in sacred onsen, cross mountain ranges, worship in dozens of temples, and often conclude the pilgrimage at Japan's most sacred waterfall, Nachi no Taki Falls.

FULL-BLOWN PILGRIMAGES

Commitment: Several months. Everyone should do this sort of pilgrimage at least once in their lives. When you take off for several months or even several years, you really figure out just who you are. There will be points along the way when you may honestly wonder if it will ever end . . . And when you come back, you'll be able to draw upon this empowering experience for the rest of your life.

Here are a couple popular examples of full-blown pilgrimages.

TREKKING THE APPALACHIAN TRAIL, EAST COAST OF THE UNITED STATES

Distance: 2,175-mile jaunt from Georgia to Maine
Duration: a good, solid five to six months of backpacking

Perhaps the most celebrated long-distance hike in the world, the Appalachian Trail hosts tens of thousands of pilgrims every year. Most pilgrims hike for just a day or two, which is one of the nicest things about this journey/shrine; you can make it whatever sort of journey you want: pico, midrange, or full-blown. Those who complete the journey are welcomed into a select order of "thru-hikers."

TREKKING THE CONTINENTAL DIVIDE TRAIL, WESTERN UNITED STATES

Distance: 3,100 miles
Duration: about six months of hiking or two or three months of mountain biking

Like its East Coast cousin, the Continental Divide Trail is a very long jaunt, crossing deserts and mountain ranges, cresting high passes, and meandering through spectacular scenery. It follows the Continental Divide through five western states (Montana, Idaho, Wyoming, Colorado, and New Mexico), running from the Canadian border down to Mexico. It doesn't have quite the following of the Appalachian Trail (in fact, only a handful of hearty pilgrims "thru-hike" every year), but completing the journey is no less an accomplishment. The Appalachian Trail, the Pacific Crest Trail, and the Continental Divide Trail—North America's premiere long-distance trails—are all examples of pilgrimages where the journey really is the shrine. No temple or sacred site awaits you at the end, just the elation of knowing you did it.

PILGRIMAGE TO THE SHWEDAGON PAGODA, MYANMAR (BURMA)

Distance: varies

Duration: several weeks to several months

The Shwedagon Pagoda in Myanmar is one of the tallest religious buildings in the world at 326 feet and one of the most magnificent; it is entirely covered in gold. Every year pilgrims make the trek by the thousands from all over Myanmar and beyond, adding tiny portions of gold leaf to the pagoda at the end of their journeys as a testament of faith. Many of these pilgrims make only pennies a day, so saving up for a piece of gold leaf to add to the pagoda may take years. Start your pilgrimage in a rural village in the northern part of the country and travel with a little family making the journey for the first time. You can pilgrimage for several weeks by foot to Shwedagon, chatting with fellow pilgrims of all stripes throughout the duration of the quest. This is one pilgrimage where the path is not defined (each quest begins at the pilgrim's front door), though each path eventually ends at the pagoda.

PLOTTING THE PATH

Perhaps you've selected a shrine that means something to you, so now it's time to plan the journey. Who will come with you? Will you go by foot or bike or something else? Throw out the maps, select your magical tokens, and let the quest take shape.

WHO WILL JOIN THE QUEST?

Choosing who will come with you on your pilgrimage is probably the most important decision you'll make. The right fellow pilgrim can enhance the quest like nothing else, while a mismatched pilgrim can be a real drag. Here are some thoughts on selecting fellow pilgrims.

1. Once you decide to go on a pilgrimage, the right person will appear. Plan the journey and see what happens.
2. If you end up going alone, embrace it. Sometimes a solo journey is exactly what a pilgrim needs, even if you find yourself resisting.
3. Every pilgrim who goes boldly forward is given a pinch of the Magic. The Magic is the pilgrim's power to work those little miracles along the way (more on this later). Go forward and the Magic will ensure that you never walk alone.

© Photo by Marla Aufmuth

THE WAY OF THE PILGRIM

There are myriad ways to go. Here are a few possibilities.

BY BIKE

Mountain or road biking is one of the best modes of pilgrimage. You can travel twelve or two hundred miles in a day; it's up to you. You're completely autonomous but still connected to people. Throwing your leg over your bike is a great feeling, like an old-West hero kicking his leg over the saddle and blazing outta town. It's also nice to know that if you hit a place you don't like you can leave quick, like a bizarre valley we came across in Scotland that was overrun by rabbits (They were everywhere! One bunny is cute, but 1,000? 10,000! It was a cheesy horror film in the making.) The only drawback is stashing your bike when you want to explore on foot.

The exhilaration of the bike-bound pilgrimage (near Avon, Montana)

BY FOOT

Walking connects you directly with the people and the land. It's also the oldest form of pilgrimage. When you walk, you're connecting with a tradition as old as humanity. Walking or backpacking allows for easier transit on buses and trains, but you don't have the same amount of freedom as you have on a bike to simply move on quickly by your own power.

"He's the walking man
Born to walk
Walk on walking man . . ."
> —James Taylor

BY THUMB

There is no better way to meet a wealth of colorful characters than by hitchhiking. Instincts are key, though. Often the roughest-looking characters are the most hospitable and kind. Be alert to your first impressions and the vibe you get when offered a ride.

BY SKATE

While biking across America, Jared, Clint, and I were three days behind a cross-country Rollerblader. I've never done it, but I'm sure it's a blast.

BY FULL-BODY PROSTRATIONS

Unless you are atoning for the sins of seven or eight lifetimes, full-body prostration is not recommended. The Tibetan Buddhists do it when they circumambulate Mount Kailash. It takes them as long as several weeks to go thirty-two miles.

BY PADDLE

A pilgrim friend, Richard Jones, rowed solo across the Atlantic. He was pretty wiped out after the two-month odyssey, but returned with a ton of stories and a super tan. Sailing, canoeing, and kayaking are also terrific options.

BY SKI

Cross-country skiing is a great way to explore otherwise inaccessible regions and have a meditative, introspective quest. A little snow, a distant shrine, and you're all set for a cross-country ski pilgrimage. A few years ago my friend Hilmar skied across Iceland's (and Europe's) largest glacier, Vatnajokll. What a workout! And what fun!

BY ENGINE

For some pilgrims, the motorcycle or car is the only way to go. If you're in debate at all, though, try a muscle-powered pilgrimage first. When you earn every inch, you tend to glean more transcendence from the journey and feel more connected to humanity. My friend Gary Kelley swears by the motorcycle pilgrimage. He toured

Everything You Need for the Harley-bound Pilgrimage:

sunglasses

gloves

Poodle (Schatzi)

Clint traded his mountain bike for a Harley during our trip across America.

Then again, maybe a hot-air balloon pilgrimage? However you decide to go, just go.

America for four months after a tough divorce. It became the key journey of his life.

MAGICAL TOKENS

Every road trip pilgrim should have a magical token of the quest. When you apply the concept of magic realism (the pilgrim's power to transform the ordinary into the enchanted) to objects, you can create magical tokens out of anything.

When Jared, Clint, and I biked from Venice Beach, California, to Springfield, Massachusetts, to the Basketball Hall of Fame, we brought along an unblemished, official NBA basketball that we asked heroic folks across America to sign.

This Hero's Ball was never played with, but sat in the cool darkness of the "Ark of the Covenant" (our bike trailer), waiting to be called upon when a heroic soul crossed our path. It symbolized what we were after on our journey: a true connection with our people and our country.

Biking to Jack and Dan's Tavern in Spokane, Washington, we carried the Golden Chalice. By drinking from the Golden Chalice at Jack and Dan's, we would be imbued with Stockton-esque basketball brilliance. We all drank from the Chalice and have not missed a jump shot since.

In Tibet, pilgrims are given a prayer scarf or *khata* before they depart for their shrine. The scarf is believed to bring good fortune throughout the journey.

For a pilgrimage to Machu Picchu, my brother Jared and I wore turquoise rings bought a month before for five bucks in Austin, Nevada. The rings became our khata of sorts, especially when Andean fireflies crawled across them and they lit up. The rings were imbued with some deep magic ever after. (But, like most magic rings, they were lost soon after the end of the journey.)

A bike trailer becomes the Ark of the Covenant; a gaudy, spray-painted glass with glue-gunned studs becomes a chalice; cheap turquoise rings become magic rings.

You can create magical tokens out of anything.

UTTERLY UNNECESSARY (BUT COMPLETELY INDISPENSABLE) STUFF TO BRING ALONG

As a pilgrim, you don't have to be the every-ounce-counts adventurer. Half the stuff you bring along may not save your life (or your time) but it could enhance the journey, and isn't that what it's all about?

Now for the stuff you might not think of.

BASKETBALL

. . . or soccer ball or football; there is no better way to liven up the journey than to shoot around or get an impromptu game going with the locals. No matter where you go in the world, sports like soccer, basketball, and volleyball are a language understood by nearly everyone.

A lad in South America poses with his soccer ball.

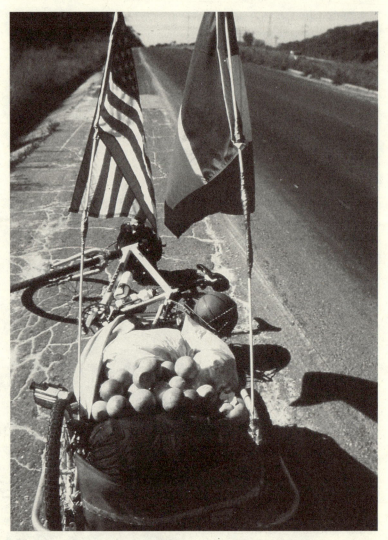

The Ark of the Covenant loaded up with oranges during my pilgrimage through Mexico

Kids play volleyball on a dirt court near Lake Tonlé Sap in Cambodia.

CAMCORDER

A camcorder can be a fun enhancement to the adventure, and maybe you'll even be inspired to put together a pilgrim documentary when you get home.

FLAGS

We've flown the flags of our host countries during several bike-bound pilgrimages. It's great to see people's reactions to their flags, and it makes pilgrims more visible and photogenic.

HAMMOCK

A relaxing alternative to your camp mat (if you have one).

MUSIC

Compose the sound track for your pilgrimage as you go along! A harmonica is a logical choice for many pilgrims; Jared serenaded us on every trip. He's now added at least five songs to his repertoire. Pilgrims toting guitars are often the hit of the campsite.

JOURNAL

Keeping a journal is one of the best ways to process the journey as well as a great way to document the adventure.

LITERATURE

Bring along some inspiring books by and about other pilgrims and pilgrimages. Some of my favorites are: *On the Road* by Jack Kerouac, *A Walk Across America* by Peter Jenkins, *Cathedrals of the Flesh* by Alexia Brue, *The Motorcycle Diaries* by Ernesto Che Guevara, *Zen and the Art of*

Motorcycle Maintenance by Robert Pirsig, *The Adventures of Huckleberry Finn* by Mark Twain, *Desert Solitaire* by Edward Abbey. Or try some poetry; give Jacques Prévert, Walt Whitman, Archibald MacLeish, and Uncle Gary a try.

MAGICAL TOKENS

Be sure to bring the aforementioned Hero's Ball, prayer scarf, Golden Chalice, magic rings, or maybe a vial of water from the ocean or a spring—whatever makes sense to you and enhances the journey.

PUSH-UP HANDLES

We dragged these things all the way across America. That's three and a half months with push-up handles clanging off the back of our bikes. They're great to have if there's no grass and you suddenly *must* do push-ups (which, as I'll show later is bound to happen, especially when chronicling your road trip pilgrim physique on film for posterity). Push-up handles can prove invaluable when you want to look especially ripped flexing at the summit sign after climbing a tough pass.

SKETCH PAD

Claim some alone time on the journey to sketch the strange and exotic locales you're passing through.

TEA KETTLE

For those long spells huddled against the rain . . . But always wait for the coals! One day we stuck our trusty tea kettle Alvin on the coals before the fire went down and it melted his lip. Alvin was Al'in ever after.

THE PILGRIM'S LEXICON

Here are a few terms referred to throughout.

Heroic Expression is the pure expression of the heart. When you seek, love, or create heroically, you are practicing Heroic Expression. Acts of Heroic Expression lead a person to her or his heroic self. Every pilgrimage can be an act of Heroic Expression, no matter where you are going, no matter how long it takes. The only thing that matters is that it matters to you.

Heroic Identity is a person's true, heroic self as well as the spiritual destination of the pilgrimage. It exists no matter how much clutter a person may have accumulated on top of it. A pilgrimage is a great way to de-clutter your heroic identity.

The Inward Journey is an act of love or creation, like writing a novel or figuring out an algorithm or just loving someone. **The outward journey** is just that: a physical journey that takes you somewhere. Keeping a journal or drawing in a sketchbook can be a powerful ritual on a pilgrimage because it allows you to engage in the inward and outward journey simultaneously. Every journey, inward or outward, can be an act of Heroic Expression, leading the pilgrim closer to his or her heroic identity.

A Key Journey is the centering journey of a person's life. Key journeys usually come at a turning point, often spinning that person's life into a new, unexpected direction. You may look back for years to come and demarcate your life from that one, powerful pilgrimage. A person may take several key journeys, but usually there's one in particular that really resonates. For me, it was my bike trip across America.

Magical Realism in this book's context refers to the pilgrim's power to transform the everyday into the magical.

Pico-Pilgrimage is a short journey with the characteristics of a longer one; in other words, a pilgrimage that incorporates transformational power, a shrine, and great fun. A pico-pilgrimage may be as brief as an afternoon or a weekend.

The Universal Joy Principal states that it is wise to make decisions that pump the most amount of joy back into the universe. The Universal Joy Principal comes in very useful on a pilgrimage; when you find yourself faced with a choice, simply apply the principle by asking what decision will bring about the most amount of overall joy. The answer (and your actions) will then naturally lead to happiness and fulfillment.

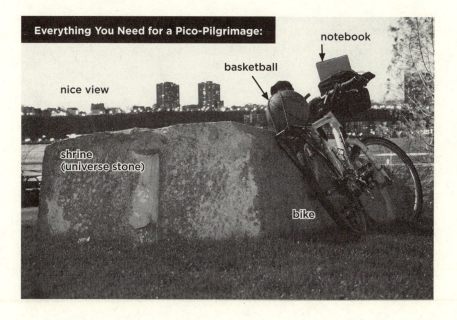

Everything You Need for a Pico-Pilgrimage:

notebook

basketball

nice view

shrine
(universe stone)

bike

CHAPTER 2
The Journey Begins

A YEAR IN SOUTH AMERICA WITH
MARLA AND BIG MAMA

"In early 1999 I found myself with a perplexing question: what should I do with my life? I'd been living in San Francisco since the early 1990s, feasting on the bounty of the dot-com industry without giving my life's direction much thought. When the digital

© *Photo by Marla Aufmuth*

well began to run dry, I realized that, at twenty-eight years old, I had no idea where to go and what to do with myself. I knew that I was at a crossroads and that my decisions at that point would profoundly influence the next phase of my life.

"One day I had an epiphany: a cultural journey was what I needed. How better to help me in finding a direction for my life than to experience the way other people live? And, if I could present myself with some personal challenges along the way, then perhaps I could break free from the day-to-day ease that I had become so accustomed to.

"My girlfriend Marla and I converted my Toyota pickup into a camper and spent a year of our lives on the road. We headed toward the southern tip of Argentina. South America seemed the perfect destination for culture and adventure. Marla and I spent the following year living in our truck, "Big Mama," exploring untouched lands, amazing cultures, and of course, ourselves.

"In those twelve months I learned more about who I was than I ever could have imagined. My pilgrimage through South America was a journey through my own soul and gave me the direction I was looking for."

— *Bart Higgins, brand strategist,*
Brooklyn, New York

AFOOT and light-hearted I take to the open road,
Healthy, free, the world before me,
The long brown path before me, leading wherever I choose.
Henceforth I ask not good-fortune, I myself am good-fortune,
Henceforth I whimper no more, postpone no more, need nothing,
Done with indoor complaints, libraries, querulous criticisms,
Strong and content, I travel the open road.
— Walt Whitman, from Song of the Open Road

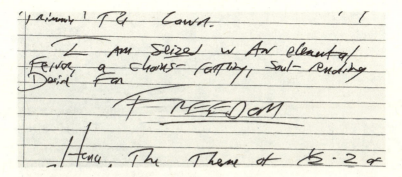

Journal entry from August 3, 2000, on a pilgrimage through Scotland and Ireland

HEADING OUT

With the preparations (if any) finished, the hour has come and it is time to head out. You can begin your pilgrimage from anywhere you want. Most journeys begin at home with that first step out the front door.

© Photo by Bart Higgins

When we biked across America, we launched from Venice Beach in Los Angeles, leaping into the ocean, playing a few games on the famous b-ball courts, and then riding east.

The ocean is a terrific place to start, and the only place if you're going coast-to-coast.

The foot of a great mountain is another good starting point. As you walk away, watch the mountain recede behind you; and when you return from the journey, watch it appear in the sky before you, welcoming you home. Wherever and however you choose to depart, you'll feel exhilarated as the journey begins (and possibly a bit overwhelmed, if it's a longer quest). With this heightened sense of reality, glance back as you ride or walk away and imagine your old self waving from where you left him, because when you go on a pilgrimage, you're never the same again.

THE PILGRIM'S MANTLE

As you embark on your journey, put on the **pilgrim's mantle**. The pilgrim's mantle is a sense of newness that accompanies the pilgrim at the beginning of the quest. It places the past behind you and helps you see the magical all around you.

How to put on the pilgrim's mantle:

1. Clear the slate. No matter what happened before, leave it all behind. Girlfriend dumped you? Forget about it. Lost your job? Gone. Couldn't finish that five-pound Big Judd burger and thus blew your chance to get your picture on the wall of fame? Over it. When you set off on the journey, you start with a clean slate.
2. Look forward. It is impossible to look forward and backward at the same time, physically or spiritually, so look forward. Look down the road and imagine where your journey will lead you.
3. Soak up the joy of being on the road.

THE FIRST FEW DAYS ON THE ROAD

MEETING THE GURU

The first encounter of the hero-journey is with a protective figure (often a little old crone or old man) who provides the adventurer with amulets against the dragon forces he is about to pass.

> — *from* The Hero with a Thousand Faces
> *by Joseph Campbell*

It happens on every quest: the hero meets a wise being, often in disguise, who imparts great wisdom and blessings on the pilgrim for the journey ahead. Philosophers have discussed this archetype for centuries. But it isn't just a convention of myth or storytelling; it happens in real life, too.

This powerful figure often appears within the first few days of the journey. You might not recognize the guru at first; he or she may simply seem like an interesting character. The guru will then disclose who he really is. He will reveal his **heroic identity**, not who he is in the limited terms of social position or class but who he really is. A pilgrimage is a great way to uncover not only others' heroic identities but your own as well. On this kind of a journey the usual encumbrances of social structure and comparative measures of lesser and greater are left behind. When you're a pilgrim, you're classless, neither above nor below anybody else. Whether dirt-poor or filthy rich, as a road trip pilgrim you can attain a

Usually the guru will look just like anybody else. It's a test, you see!
Any of these people could be your guru. You just never know.

sort of freedom not easily maintained in daily life. Carrying back this new perspective to your daily life when the journey is complete is one of the great gifts of the pilgrimage.

During our journey across America, we camped out our first night at a churchyard in Pasadena, California. In the morning, the church caretaker allowed us not only to stay, but to wash up. We asked him to sign our Hero's Ball, the magic token of the journey. He signed his name *Rev K. Shaw*. We asked him what the "Rev" meant, and he said it meant reverend. The caretaker was actually the reverend! The guru in disguise. And in that moment of recognition, the caretaker transformed before us, standing taller, eyes radiating light. He gave us this bit of wisdom for the trek ahead: "Seek a friend before you need a friend," which was exactly what we were trying to do. Embrace America and humanity. Then he blessed our journey, "God bless you all and a safe journey." This blessing would stay with us for 4,800 miles.

It wasn't until we saw him for who he was that he shrugged off his "disguise" and became the guru, like Hera in Greek mythology disguising herself as an old woman to see if the hero Jason would carry her on his back across the river, then blessing him after he did.

In the prologue to this book, I think you'll find an unlikely guru in disguise who teaches me a valuable lesson that enhances the rest of my journey.

DONATING TO THE LOCAL ECONOMY WITHOUT EVEN REALIZING IT

Just as meeting the guru is a given on your pilgrimage, it is also inevitable that you will endure a few screwups, especially during the first few days when you're getting used to life on the road. To unwittingly make a donation to the local economy, do the following:

Step 1. Forget to button down the tarp on your Ark (bike trailer) or the flap on your backpack. This will ensure that something will fall out.

Step 2. Choose a bumpy stretch of road or trail. This will help it fall out more quickly.

Step 3.   A few miles down the road, check the trailer or your pack and see how things are going in there. If you've followed the directions, you should have lost something by now.

PowerBar gave me a whole ton of bars and gel for my 1,500-mile bike pilgrimage through Mexico. I brought them all and packed them into a backpack that I stuck in the back of the Ark. The backpack probably topped forty pounds; I was not going hungry on this quest.

A few miles down the road I pulled over to take a break and noticed I had forgotten to button down the Ark, and the backpack was gone. I can only imagine that some humble Mexican family, having just said their prayers and facing certain hunger, was ambling innocently down the road when they found this bulging backpack sitting there as if it had fallen from heaven.

Which leads me to this little parable:

THE PARABLE OF THE PEAR

On a pico-pilgrimage one day, I was walking down a sidewalk when suddenly I was stopped dead in my tracks. Hanging right before me, right over this heavily trafficked sidewalk in a major American city, was a pear.

It was the ripest, juiciest pear I have ever seen. It was so fat it might have fallen off the branch any second. The branch was completely bent over, this pear was so huge. And the crazy thing about it was that the branch was angled perfectly over the sidewalk so that the pear literally hung within inches of my head. The situation could not have been more ideal.

So I just stared at this pear for a few moments. How in the world had this pear, hanging there in the height of ripeness, not been picked? It was baffling and unlikely, but there it was. So I reached up and I plucked the pear off the tree. And it came off the branch without any resistance, as if this were the very moment it had been made for.

And then I ate that pear as I walked along. It was the juiciest, sweetest pear I have ever had. And I marveled again that it was there. For me.

This is how it works on a pilgrimage: The unexpected, but perfectly timed little miracles of the road will be waiting for you, right when you arrive.

CHAPTER 3
Camping on a Pilgrimage

THE FREMONT RIVER TRAIL

"Every year I make a pilgrimage to Capitol Reef National Park in southeastern Utah. My favorite spot in Capitol Reef is the summit of the Fremont River Trail, which begins in Fruita campground, wanders alongside the rust-colored Fremont River, and then ascends to an altarlike pinnacle of red sandstone overlooking the

park's majestic cliffs and canyons. I like to hike that trail at sunset and watch the blue desert sky fade to black, revealing a canopy of brilliant white stars. The beauty of that spot is its deep silence and the sweeping view of the red cliffs with the tiny settlement at their base. As I sit at the summit looking at the park's magnificent natural beauty, I feel safe and peaceful. Somehow, all the superficial trappings of life are suddenly stripped away, and I am home."

— Michael Chipman, concert vocalist,
Salt Lake City, Utah

FINDING A FREE PLACE TO CAMP

Lord knows, there's nothing more important on a pilgrimage than finding a place to rest your head after a long day on the road. And with a road trip pilgrim's typically limited resources, finding a free place most nights is essential. Here are some tips on how to camp for free without getting the boot.

:: **Choose sites that are a bit off the beaten path.** Suburban parks are a better bet than downtown parks, even in smaller towns.

:: **Churchyards are almost always good,** though you may get the occasional pastor who will object.

:: **Set up camp after dark**, once most folks have gone to bed.

:: **If caught, employ the great pilgrim mantra,** "We rolled in real late last night."

:: **Befriend locals at community events.** Often people will take an interest in the quest and invite you to stay over or at least camp in their yard.

PILGRIM TIP

Always scout out the sprinkler system when setting up camp. There is nothing more annoying than getting doused in the middle of the night with cold water. (For types of sprinklers and disarmament techniques, see Chapter 6.)

GREAT PILGRIM CAMPSITES

The following list is by no means exhaustive, but it represents some of our great finds over the years and will hopefully inspire you in your quest for cheap (better yet, free) sleep on your pilgrimage.

CAMPSITE RATING SYSTEM

Generally, three factors go into choosing the best campsites for pilgrims; I have given each locale below a rating of **Low or Nonexistent, Medium,** or **High** for each of the factors. It is assumed that these campsites will be free, so price is not factored in.

1. The cool factor. Lighthouses and beaches score high on the cool factor; the side of the road generally scores low. Campsites scoring high on the cool factor are those that inspire you with great vistas, have benefits like on-site natural hot springs, or just make for great stories. How many people have camped in a castle, for instance?

2. Comfort and amenities. Is there grass? Is it soft? Are there bathrooms? Running water? Basketball courts? Small-town parks often score high on the comfort factor, as the grass is generally soft, the

Typical Pilgrim's Camp

Jared over here somewhere playing the harmonica

soccer goals: camping in soccer field

me

flag

sunglasses

fellow pilgrim (Clint)

tent

books

Hero's ball hidden in Ark

sleeping bag

sludge pot

bike panniers

note: camp in shaggier softer grass

thermos

Ark of the Covenant

dirty clothes

push up handles

basketball

sprinkler! (disarm before bed)

bathrooms are generally open, and potable water is readily available. Golf courses also score high (sleeping on the greens is very comfortable *and* good for the back), while lighthouses and castles score low (scraggly grass, no bathrooms, no water) even though they're very cool.

3. Possibility of getting kicked out. National capitals score high (try pitching your tent on the White House lawn and getting away with it); churches score low (it's unusual to be kicked off a church lawn).

Here's my list of recommended pilgrim campsites in order of availability, with the most common campsites listed first. You'll stumble across quite a few churches on a pilgrimage and an infinite number of possible roadside camps, but probably few ski resorts or drive-in movie theaters.

Side of the road
Churches
Town parks
Campgrounds
Hurling fields and other athletic grounds
Picnic areas
Golf courses
Banana plantations and other agricultural fields
The beach
Cemeteries
Airports
Desert plateaus
Mountaintops
Roundabouts
Drive-in movie theaters
Lighthouses
Castles
Temples
Tundra
Tepees
Ski resorts

SIDE OF THE ROAD

In rural areas it's not a bad way to go, especially if the roadsides have grass. We camped right beneath a guardrail on a nice patch of grass next to a highway in Indiana. Another time we camped on a dirt-road turnout going up a pass in Colorado. We built a little wall of piled-up rocks to keep the Jeeps from plowing our tent into the river during the night if they didn't make the turn.

Cool factor: Low to Medium
Comfort and amenities: Low
Possibility of getting kicked out: Low

CHURCHES

Aside from Catholic churches, which tend to be the least welcoming to pilgrims sleeping on their property, virtually all other denominations (Methodist, Lutheran, Unitarian) are pretty hospitable. We have camped out at the following churches many times in several countries with no problem. They are ranked here in terms of how many times we've camped there and our general sense of how accommodating they are:

1. Unitarians
2. Christian Scientists
3. Mormons
4. Lutherans
5. Methodists
6. Anglicans/Episcopalians
7. Baptists
8. Catholics

Cool factor: Low
Comfort and amenities: Medium (beware of sprinklers)
Possibility of getting kicked out: Low, unless you choose a Catholic church

TOWN PARKS

It's very unlikely you'll get kicked out of a small-town park, and the locals may even amble over to ask questions and give you cookies.

Pilgrim's Road-side Camp (Colorado)

Engineer Pass

wild Jeeper

dirt road

Pilgrim's journal and pen

protective wall of rocks

pot and stove

sludge fixin's

Ark of the Covenant

map

oatmeal

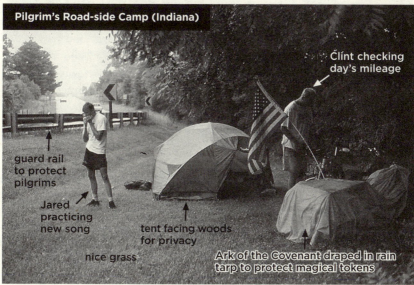

Pilgrim's Road-side Camp (Indiana)

Clint checking day's mileage

guard rail to protect pilgrims

Jared practicing new song

tent facing woods for privacy

nice grass

Ark of the Covenant draped in rain tarp to protect magical tokens

Pilgrim Town Park Camp (Mesquite, Nevada)

See if you can find Jared writing in his journal . . .

Clint still asleep . . .

tent set up on soft grass with nice view of baseball field

peanut butter ready to go

Remember, small-town folks are always looking for something interesting to break up the quiet. Three pilgrims with bikes and flags—cool! Where are they going? Where have they been? You'll get in the paper and you'll be the talk of the town. You may even get invited over for dinner. Small-town parks usually have well-kept bathrooms; comfy, well-tended grass; and running water as well. Small *tourist-town* parks, however, are a different story. Local law enforcement may kick you out or move you elsewhere.

Cool factor: Medium

Comfort and amenities: High (beware of sprinklers)

Possibility of getting kicked out: Low, unless it's a tourist town

CAMPGROUNDS

Sometimes the amenities of a campground outweigh the price. See below for ways to evade campground fees. Some campgrounds, such as the New Brighton Beach campground in Capitola, California, are well worth the price. New Brighton is perched on a cliff above the ocean with easy beach access, and there are even reduced-fee sites for pilgrims. It's a favorite stop for PCH (Pacific Coast Highway) road trippers. National-park campgrounds have a nice feeling of community and often have discounts for pilgrims.

Cool factor: Low to High

Comfort and amenities: High

Possibility of getting kicked out: Medium, if you don't pay

HURLING FIELDS AND OTHER ATHLETIC GROUNDS

In Ireland they play this sport called hurling. The fields are lush and it's great entertainment to boot. Soccer fields, cricket pitches, the outfield of baseball fields, and football stadiums make for great campsites as well. Beware the proud caretaker and be careful not to burn a crop circle in his well-tended grass with your camp stove.

Near Glasgow, Scotland. Look at all the space we got! It's the freakin' Marriott tonight, boys!

Cool factor: Medium

Comfort and amenities: Medium (beware of sprinklers)

Possibility of getting kicked out: Generally low

PICNIC AREAS

Picnic areas make great campsites. You'll have the place to yourself, the grass will be soft, and there will likely be running water and toilets. Just be sure to roll in late, set up camp late, and position your tent in a shadowy area away from an easily visible road. Sometimes park rangers, camp hosts, and cops do cursory inspections of picnic areas, often just driving by to make sure nothing's up. If you find a clever place to camp and set up late, you should be fine. We have successfully camped in many picnic areas,

Classic Picnic Area Camp

bathroom and tables over here

tents secluded in trees hidden from road

soft brush to sleep on

though one time at Lake Mead, Nevada, we had a run-in with a diabolical camp host hell-bent on making us sorry for our picnic-site piracy (luckily, we set up camp late the night before and he found us in the morning when the deed was already done). We have only been evicted once though, and that was in Yellowstone National Park.

Cool factor: Low

Comfort and amenities: High (disarm the sprinklers)

Possibility of getting kicked out: Low, if you're wily

GOLF COURSES

It's quite a task to build a golf course. The putting greens are typically composed of several inches of sand beneath the surface of the grass, providing that dense, cushioned feeling. It's great for putting and even better for sleeping. Take a snooze on the green and get up for a 7:00 AM tee time. Just make sure you set up late and pack up early. (Golf-course camping is also quite good for realigning the pilgrim's strained back.)

Cool factor: Medium

Comfort and amenities: High (disarm the sprinklers)
Possibility of getting kicked out: Medium, about 50/50

BANANA PLANTATION AND OTHER AGRICULTURAL FIELDS

In the summer, you can burrow away among the cornstalks or deep inside the banana or sugarcane fields. In the winter, fallow fields make a nice place to camp.

Cool factor: Medium
Comfort and amenities: Low
Possibility of getting kicked out: Low

THE BEACH

The best campsite of all, I'd say. We camped two nights on the busiest beach weekend of the year (Labor Day) at one of the busiest beaches on the East Coast (the Jersey Shore near Seaside Heights) and didn't get kicked out. We chose a plot of sand against a dune so people couldn't

Camping out on the New Jersey shore

see us, set up late, and when the cops came roaring up to boot us out on night two, they were so intrigued by the tales we spun from our quest, we could have camped out for a month.

In Ireland we camped on the beach at Rosslare Harbor, waiting for the next day's ferry to Wales. No problem at all, pilgrims do it all the time there. In Brazil I slept on Copacabana Beach in Rio de Janeiro one night in November. Nobody bothered me. Rest of the world . . . we've camped on the beach any chance we could and rarely had trouble.

Cool factor: High

Comfort and amenities: Medium

Possibility of getting kicked out: Low, but depends on the popularity of the beach

CEMETERIES

Not as creepy as you'd think. Rural cemeteries are often situated on hills with nice views, and cops rarely patrol them. Larger town and city

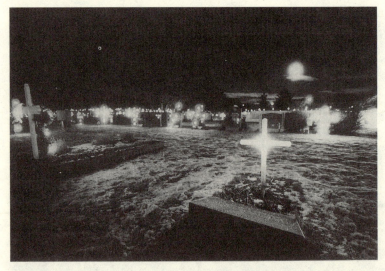

Cemeteries in Scandinavia, like this one in Gullfoss, Iceland, are lit up at Christmastime, making it even more fun to camp there.

cemeteries are not as ideal because cops do patrol these. So stick to the small-town graveyards, and you'll be fine. In Europe small-town church-yards (which generally double as graveyards) are also quite good.

Cool factor: Medium

Comfort and amenities: Medium (beware of sprinklers)

Possibility of getting kicked out: Small cemetery: low; larger one: medium

AIRPORTS

Camping *outside* an airport on that no-man's-land by the runway can be risky, but it is pretty cool to kick back and watch those massive hulks of metal roar by a hundred feet overhead. And what pilgrim hasn't camped out *inside* the airport on a long layover?

Outside the airport near the runway:

Cool factor: High

Comfort and amenities: Low

Possibility of getting kicked out: High

Heathrow airport camp, London

Inside the airport:

Cool factor: Low

Comfort and amenities: Medium

Possibility of getting kicked out: Low

DESERT PLATEAUS

A great place to commune with the stars, the sky, and the earth. Camping in the desert is one of the most soul-centering things a pilgrim can do. You know no one's going to bother you (unless you've crossed a desert hermit; more on that in chapter 6), and you can fall asleep mesmerized by the massive chunks of glittering stars that hang seemingly inches above your head.

Cool factor: High

Comfort and amenities: Low

Possibility of getting kicked out: Nonexistent

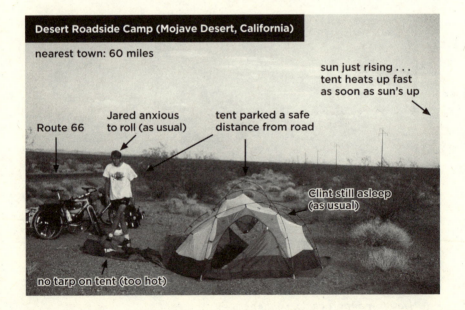

Desert Roadside Camp (Mojave Desert, California)

nearest town: 60 miles

sun just rising . . . tent heats up fast as soon as sun's up

Route 66

Jared anxious to roll (as usual)

tent parked a safe distance from road

Clint still asleep (as usual)

no tarp on tent (too hot)

MOUNTAINTOPS

If it's not too windy and the weather's nice, camping on a mountaintop can be inspiring and restful, especially if you have a view. My brothers and sisters and I camped on top of the Hero's Mountain a couple times over New Year's, made a roaring fire, and chatted all night long. I've camped out on mountains and hills on several pilgrimages, and on the Fourth of July to watch fireworks.

Cool factor: High

Comfort and amenities: Low

Possibility of getting kicked out: Nonexistent

Mountaintop camp in the highlands of Scotland

ROUNDABOUTS

No one will expect you to camp here, in the middle of the road; just make sure there's enough cover. Roundabouts are definitely not for the pilgrim seeking a good night's sleep; they're more for fun or possibly for desperate situations when you can't find anything else.

Cool factor: Medium

Comfort and amenities: Low

Possibility of getting kicked out: Medium, if you're visible

DRIVE-IN MOVIE THEATERS

Choose a nice patch of grass in the back of the lot. Kick back and enjoy the movie. When the show's over, make friends with the projectionist, probably some college student who'll think you can walk on water for traveling so far. Maybe you'll even score some free popcorn. The projectionist will tell you that he couldn't care less if you crash here, but the owner is the one to worry about. He'll give you all the info you need,

Drive-In campsite, Kearney, Nebraska

like "That's his house right over there, so don't camp in the open." Or, "He usually swings by around 9:00 AM, so be off before then." Thank the projectionist and enjoy your night out under the stars at one of the great, iconic American places.

Cool factor: High

Comfort and amenities: Low

Possibility of getting kicked out: Low, if you're careful

LIGHTHOUSES

Not only do lighthouses offer great views but, in my experience, lighthouse keepers love a little company to break up the monotony of their jobs. A word of caution though: if it is foggy or looks like it might become so, don't camp next to the foghorn. Doing so will lead to a very long night.

Cape Wrath lighthouse in northern Scotland

Cool factor: High
Comfort and amenities: Medium
Possibility of getting kicked out: Low (especially since most lighthouses are automated these days)

CASTLES

About as cool for ambience as you get, though sometimes a bit creepy. On one pilgrimage through Scotland, Jared, Micah, and I spied a castle on a hill in the distance, turned down a country road, and pitched our tents in the front yard. While our pot of sludge bubbled away, Jared found a historical plaque recounting a story about the owner of the place and the fifty or so people he killed there in the sixteenth century, right on the spot where we stood. The castle, as the plaque described, has apparently been haunted ever since. Jared was creeped out for the rest of the night and none of us slept very well.

Cool factor: High

Comfort and amenities: Low (even lower if it's haunted)

Possibility of getting kicked out: Low to medium; depends on the castle (and the ghosts)

TEMPLES

All over Asia, temple monks will put you up for the night, especially in rural areas. They may ask for a small donation, but it's usually within any pilgrim's

Mountaintop temple in Cambodia

budget (and while skirting camp fees is advocated later in this chapter, weaseling out of the two-dollar temple donation is just bad karma).

Cool factor: High

Comfort and amenities: Varies; Low to High

Possibility of getting kicked out: Low

TUNDRA

You'll come across tundra at high altitudes and in the far Northern and Southern Hemispheres. Alpine tundra, unlike Arctic or Antarctic tundra,

Colorado high country

does not exist atop a layer of permafrost and so can actually be fairly comfortable to sleep on. Make sure to find a little hollow to set up the tent in, to block the frequent winds.

Cool factor: Medium

Comfort and amenities: Low

Possibility of getting kicked out: Nonexistent

TEPEES

You may stumble across a tepee in the Western United States. We camped in a tepee one night on our way to Spokane.

Cool factor: Medium

Comfort and amenities: Low

Possibility of getting kicked out: Medium; depends on the tepee

OK, so it's not an authentic tepee, but it was fun (southern Idaho).

SKI RESORTS

In the summertime there's something serene and surreal about camping at the top of a ski resort. You can sit on the quiet chairlift. You can gaze out over mountain vistas. And, since ski resorts have lots of open space for their runs, finding a place to pitch your tent, a good supply of firewood, and a nice view shouldn't be a problem.

Cool factor: High
Comfort and amenities: Medium
Possibility of getting kicked out: Low

PILGRIM CAMPSITES IN THE BIG CITY

About big cities: if you hit one on your pilgrimage and you're broke, here are some possible places to crash for the night.

A BUSY PUBLIC SPACE

Hard to believe, but a busy public space like a square or monument is a good bet. Make sure it is lit up all night and pretty active. Just hang out, write, and watch the passing of life. Sleep in shifts. This doesn't make for a very good night's sleep, but it can be fun. Busy places like Columbus Circle in New York City work well for this. And, you never know, someone may end up inviting you over.

A PARK

Camp right out in the open; don't try to hide. You'll be safer in the open, at least that's what we've concluded. Be sure to set up camp late, after law enforcement passes through.

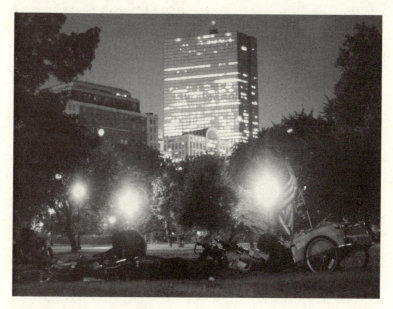

Our campsite in Boston Common

THE SUBWAY

Not easy with bikes, but reliable and warmish. Some subways (like New York) are open 24-7, so if you're desperate for a place to stick out the night (and can fork over a couple bucks for subway fare), then you have a relatively warm (or air-conditioned) haven until morning.

THE SUBURBS

If you have the energy and inclination, make your way out of the city and head for the closest suburb. You can usually find a secluded spot.

We've camped in Boston Common, right out in the open. Late that night a bunch of punks came through the park making a ton of noise, then suddenly one of them said: "Shh! The bikers are trying to sleep!" In Cincinnati we camped out in a dark corner of a little park on the outskirts of town, right across the street from a glittery factory. In Los Angeles we camped out in a churchyard. In Washington, DC, we tried to camp on the steps of the Lincoln Memorial, but a cute girl invited us over instead. In Baltimore we camped out in a park in the suburbs. In Paris I wandered around all night and snoozed on park benches. In London we chickened out and got a room at the youth hostel.

THE ETHICS OF PAYING THE CAMPGROUND FEE

Now if you end up bypassing all of the great free camping options for the comfort and reliability of a campground, you may find yourself cringing at the hefty fee. And not just cringing because it's expensive, but cringing because it's *unjust*. Many campgrounds charge everyone the *same fee:* from that massive RV blocking your view and drowning the sounds of the woods with its generator grinding—to you: low-impact, (often) zero-emissions pilgrim leaving the place better than you found it. Some government and private campgrounds have reduced fees for pilgrims. If your campground gives you a nice break because you're on bike or foot, pay the reduced fee. That's fair. If there are no fee reductions for pilgrims (or the reduction is only a buck or two), you may opt to take matters into your own hands.

Government campsites with pouch system:

Step-1. Pay what you can—what you feel is fair.

Step-2. Fill out the fee envelope and stub just as you would otherwise.

Step-3. Put the envelope in the receptacle as late as possible. Sometimes camp hosts count the loot nightly. This is unlikely, but if they do, they'll come over and ask for the difference.

Step-4. Boogie as early as you can. The longer you wait to get going, the greater chance you have of being caught.

Step-5. If you feel guilty later about taking the discount (and even if you don't), soothe your conscience by picking up a little extra trash along the road as you cruise along.

Private campgrounds with pay-in-person:

Step-1. Befriend the person in charge of the campground.

Step-2. Explain that you're a pilgrim and request a reduced fee.

Step-3. Negotiate something fair and pay this.

Step-4. If they won't budge, hand over the amount you believe to be fair, smile, and set up your camp. If you still get the boot, find somewhere else to camp.

I have only been confronted once, and that was on the final night of a thousand-mile bike ride down from Canada to Hyrum, Utah. Late that night, Micah, Jared, Clint, and I were relaxing around the picnic table sipping hot chocolate when a longtime family friend (who was working for one of those private organizations that collect campground fees) rolled up to collect. I guess he figured we'd just made a mistake and asked for the remaining few dollars. We explained that we were **pilgrims** and as pilgrims we didn't pay exorbitant camp fees. And you know, after a couple mugs of hot chocolate, three s'mores, a hot dog and some good tales from the road—he left!

RUN-INS WITH THE LAW

If you pilgrimage for a while, especially if you crash in parks, cemeteries, drive-ins, roadsides, and the like, it is inevitable to have a few visits from law enforcement. The trick is to welcome the cops to your campsite with the same gusto you'd welcome a bevy of Gatorade-toting masseuses. Once the cops realize that you're actually sort of happy to see them, they'll deduce that you can't possibly be doing anything wrong. And then when you wow them with stories of your epic journey, they'll be delighted to offer wisdom (like directions to a secluded, locals-only swimming hole or a diner with the town's best burgers) and even bless the campsite. We've had cops offer to swing by throughout the night on their beat just to make sure we were doing OK. Purvey a tough-guy, leave-me-the-hell-alone attitude and you'll just make things difficult for yourself, as well as curtail the possibility of actually making some unlikely allies. If you don't expect cops to be jerks, usually they won't be.

WHEN THE COPS KICK YOU OUT OF YOUR CAMPSITE

OK, so the cops have arrived at your campsite and it looks like they're going to kick you out. This is what you do:

1. Remember, you are pilgrims. Not misguided miscreants, not hapless vagabonds, but pilgrims, the noble purveyors and seekers of truth whose mantle has covered such eclectic greats as Joan of Arc, Jesus, Buddha, Henry David Thoreau, Edward Abbey, John Muir, Harriet Tubman, Muhammad, Booker T. Washington, Che Guevara, Mark Twain, Moses, Mansa Musa, John Steinbeck, Amelia Earhart, Jack Kerouac, Nelson Mandela, and Mother Teresa.

2. The cops are just doing their job of keeping their communities safe. If you're cool and convince them you're harmless, they'll probably let you stay.

3. Wow them with stories of how far you've been traveling. Cops are just like everyone else. If you're cordial and nice, chances are they'll think what you're up to is cool and leave you alone, and if that doesn't work . . .

4. Tell the cops you've always dreamed about camping at the (beach, park, hurling field, etc.). We did this in Ireland and the caretaker of a hurling field went from angry pilgrim hater to our new best friend. If that doesn't work . . .
5. Tell them you're too tired to move or you have a sprained ankle, heat exhaustion, or something. If that doesn't work . . .
6. See if the cop will relocate you somewhere else. Only once in the hundreds of nights we've camped as pilgrims did a cop kick us out of a park and offer no alternative (it happened in New Jersey). Be cool, be heroic (you are a noble pilgrim, a seeker of wisdom!) and the cops will be your friends.

ENCOUNTERS WITH CAMP HOSTS, PARK RANGERS, AND SUSPICIOUS LOCALS

Most people will find your quest quite interesting; however, if you run into a belligerent camp host, uptight park ranger, or suspicious local while camping on a pilgrimage, this is what you do:

1. Retain your pilgrim dignity. Remember number one in the previous section. You are a road trip pilgrim on a heroic quest.
2. Take an interest in where you are. Ask the suspicious camp host, park ranger, or local about his town or area. They will see that you think their kingdom is cool and will (hopefully) warm up to you.
3. Run like hell. Sometimes it's the only option, especially if you're facing a fine or jail time.

CHAPTER 4

Pilgrim Hygiene

AN EXPLORATION OF THE WORLD'S GREATEST BATHING CULTURES: FROM TURKISH HAMMAMS TO JAPANESE ONSEN

"I became obsessed with the social traditions of public bathing in the late 1990s. After visiting several of Paris's hammams, I came home to New York and started hanging out at the

Russian shvitz on the Lower East Side, the same place my great-grandfather Isadore frequented in the early twentieth century. I loved the sense of community and camaraderie of sweating with strangers, as well as the fierce yet protective warmth of the cavelike rooms. The heat and the resulting feeling of mental clarity are addictive.

"I decided that New York needed a clean, modern Turkish bath and that I, with zero business experience, was just the person to open it. This was before spas were as ubiquitous as Starbucks. Since I had no idea how to write a business plan, but some idea how to write a book proposal, I did just that. I figured that before opening my own business I needed to know everything there was to know about public baths. I was able to sell my book idea to a publisher, which funded a backpacker-style trip to see what remained of the bathing traditions I had studied and endlessly romanticized.

"I was twenty-six when I set off on my eight-month journey. I packed one small roller suitcase and a backpack. I was a tourist with a Turkish towel, spending roughly a month immersed in each bathing culture. I started my trip in Istanbul and then moved on to Greece where archaeologists were excavating a Roman bath. I then headed to Budapest, Helsinki, St. Petersburg, and Tokyo. In each place, I based myself in a city (I would find a small, cheap rental apartment a day or two after I arrived) and would roam from there, visiting public baths in the countryside. Often, I would visit up to three baths a day. In Istanbul, for example, I found various lists of still-functioning hammams, visited them all, then settled on a favorite that I kept returning to in an attempt to become a regular myself. Luckily, public baths are an affordable pleasure. In general, they cost about two to five dollars to use. In Moscow, I once paid twenty dollars at an upmarket banya, but that was the record.

"Each and every bath was completely fascinating to me, and actually became more so as the trip progressed and as my frame of reference deepened. The architecture, the history, the local rituals and grooming habits, and most of all, the people themselves told the story of this incredible practice, one that in America we've never experienced in any mainstream way. The baths, more than I ever could have imagined, were a window into each culture. Not only did I make friends at the baths, my focus also provided me access to many unusual travel experiences. After rolling into a town, I would try to get the word out that I was there to do a crash course in local bathing. This led to all sorts of introductions to people with their own deep ties to baths, whether their uncle used to own one, they were trying to renovate one, or they had memories of going every week with their mother. Having a focus meant I was never at a loss for words when traveling. I found that people liked to talk about the baths, to give me advice, and to share their memories.

"Looking back, I did incredibly little planning, and it was perfect. There was serendipity to that trip that I've never managed to recapture. Also, I was in my midtwenties and strangely, probably stupidly, fearless. When people hear about my experiences or read my book, a lot of women can't wrap their heads around traveling alone for eight months, but I can honestly say I was never lonely or wanting for company, and I never felt in danger. I felt like I was on a mission to soak up something very specific, and that sense of purpose always made me feel safe. And although I didn't realize it at the time, I returned home with a collection. Sitting down now, six years after that trip, I can close my eyes and recall picture-perfect snapshots of each of the roughly two hundred fifty baths I visited."

— *Alexia Brue, author of* Cathedrals of the Flesh: My Search for the Perfect Bath *(Bloomsbury USA, 2004), Brooklyn, New York*

Getting really dirty is one of the great benefits of going on a pilgrimage. There's something so liberating about piling on layers of sweat and dirt and not caring a bit. Eventually, however, most pilgrims yearn to be clean, if only for a few hours, and so, like finding creative places to camp, basic hygiene can become quite an adventure as well.

WHEN YOU THINK YOU NEED A SHOWER BUT CAN'T GET ONE

1. The first thing to remember is that you really don't need a shower. You're a pilgrim. You are one with the sky, the rain, the earth, the dirt. You have far loftier goals than mere cleanliness.
2. The second thing to remember is that it's fun to be sweaty. What other time in your life can you be grimy 24-7, for as long as you want, and not lose your job or your girlfriend?
3. The longer you go without a shower, the easier and more fun it becomes. You get accustomed to your filth and it's actually sort of depressing to wash it off, like saying goodbye to a friend.

4. Take pleasure in scraping off the layers of dirt. It will gross out your comrades.
5. Make scraping off dirt a spiritual experience. You, like the caterpillar, are ensconced in your dirt chrysalis, and when the layers of grime come off, you are reborn a new being. OK, this one's a bit of a stretch.
6. Go for the no-shower record among your friends. Two weeks, you say? No problem.

7. Write your pals back home
   and wow them with how
   long you've gone without a
   shower. My personal record is
   nearly four weeks without a
   shower. I did, however, jump
   in a waterfall, a lake, and
   three rivers during that time.

HOW/WHERE TO GET A FREE SHOWER ON A PILGRIMAGE

So you're way beyond the whole spirituality-of-filth thing and just really ready for a shower. Here are some tips on how to get clean for free.

1. Get a trial gym membership. Just walk into a gym, befriend the desk clerk, and see if they'll give you a free day pass. Most gyms will do this, especially if you are willing to endure their sales spiel. Never underestimate the advantage of being on a pilgrimage; people will be delighted to help you out.*

   *Folks who work for crap wages want to feel vindicated in the roles they occupy. It's what makes their job tolerable. *Yeah, I'm working for nothing, but hey, in this little kingdom, I got power.* Having been a hotel desk clerk for seven bucks an hour, I know. Somebody comes in, real hard up, you give 'em a deal. You give 'em a helluva deal. Same concept here. Give these crap-wage laborers (like front-desk folks at the gym) a chance to do something heroic, to use their power, and very often they will. And the best thing of all: you don't even have to really do anything. Just lean back on the Magic, and let things roll from there.

2. Get invited over to someone's house. Being on a pilgrimage allows you to meet all kinds of people. Eventually someone will invite you over for a home-cooked meal or a nice, hot shower or a couch to sleep on (or all three).

3. Find a beach, state park, or recreation area. Most of these places have free or coin-op showers you can use without paying camp or usage fees.

4. Sneak into a church. I was on a car-bound pilgrimage in the middle of winter one year. As usual, I had no money and nowhere to go. But there was a church in town with showers. One day, when the church was open, I found a door that nobody used and put a donation envelope between the door and frame. Late that night I snuck in. There wasn't one shower spigot, but four! And it had been fifteen-below the night before, pretty cold to sleep in your car. I thawed off for an hour with all four jets blasting. Then I went back to my car and slept. I did this for about a week before Larry, the janitor, caught me.

ALTERNATIVES TO SHOWERS

Still need a shower? Let's re-envision the shower . . .

1. **The ocean.** Think of salt water as nature's body scrub. The ocean's physical and spiritual benefits have called to pilgrims for millennia, and ocean bathing has long been esteemed in many coastal regions for its restorative properties. In the mid-nineteenth century, Biarritz, France, a onetime Viking settlement and former whaling village, became famous for its purportedly therapeutic ocean waters. Thousands made pilgrimages to the town's beaches to relax and heal.

2. **Rivers.** Always an invigorating alternative! Be sure you don't get carried away in the current.

3. **Hot springs.** Nothing better if the mix of hot and cold is right. Pilgrims to Mount Kailash know what they're talking about; following a circuit of the mountain, they enjoy a ritualistic bath at the sacred Tirthapuri hot springs. A visit to Landmannalaugar hot springs in Iceland is becoming standard fare for many visitors.

4. **Rain.** Strip down and let it soak you. Do a little rain dance in the street as you scrub off the dirt and rejoice.

5. **Sweat, exercise, and a good diet.** Sounds crazy, but you just don't need to shower as much on the road. Or, maybe we just got used to ourselves *au naturel*. Studies have shown that working out constantly and eating well makes for cleaner sweat. I can't remember where I read this, but from personal experience it does seem to hold true.

6. **Drinking fountain.** Some drinking fountains have a spigot on the bottom. Get down on the ground and spray yourself off.

7. **Sprinklers.** This is their one redeeming quality on a pilgrimage.

8. **Somebody's garden hose.** Sneak into their backyard and spray off.

9. **Somebody's swimming pool.** A real charge sneaking in, taking a dip, and getting out of there before the porch light snaps on or their Maltese starts yapping. Better yet, try a hotel pool. (While working that hotel desk job in West Yellowstone, I'd dish out the pool key to local kids and pilgrims all the time.)

10. **Sinks.** We've spent many an evening perched on the counters in restrooms soaking our feet.

11. **Coin-op car washes.** For a few quarters, you get a high-power rinse, soap, and wax sure to blast away the most ground-in grime!

12. **Fire hydrants.** Don't let inner-city kids have all the fun!

13. **Moats.** You could swim laps around the castle!

Kids swim in the moat at Angkor Wat.

14. Fountains. They're everywhere. Look for them in city plazas, business parks, city parks, casino entrances, mansion grounds, and university campuses. The water may be recirculated, but fountains are fun!

GREAT FOUNTAIN SWIMMING HOLES

We have found some great fountains on our pilgrimages The following are some of our favorites.

COLUMBUS CIRCLE FOUNTAIN, NEW YORK CITY

The serene beauty of Columbus Circle is perfectly suited for shower or romance. I saw a huge, fat pilgrim strip down and bathe for an hour beneath the arcs of water. Nobody stopped him; nobody dared.

**FOUNTAIN OF THE PLANETS AND UNISPHERE
FOUNTAIN, FLUSHING MEADOWS, QUEENS, NEW YORK**

A favorite swimming hole in the summer, until the cops come to spoil the fun.

TEN FOUNTAIN SQUARE, CINCINNATI, OHIO
Spectacular! We hit this fountain during our pilgrimage across America.

INDIANA UNIVERSITY FOUNTAIN, BLOOMINGTON, INDIANA
Is this for real? So perfect for showering pilgrims, it's unbelievable!

BUCKINGHAM FOUNTAIN, CHICAGO, ILLINOIS
Water for all!

TEMPLE SQUARE, SALT LAKE CITY, UTAH
All sorts of fun fountains. You've got about three to five minutes before security rolls up.

LAS VEGAS HOTEL FOUNTAINS, LAS VEGAS, NEVADA
More fountains than you could ever swim in for one pilgrimage (get out quick before security arrives).

JAMISON SQUARE FOUNTAIN, PORTLAND, OREGON
Practically made for bathing! And in the summertime, everybody's in the water!

INTERNATIONAL FOUNTAIN, SEATTLE CENTER, SEATTLE, WASHINGTON

At lunch hour every day, piped-in classical music complements enormous sprays, and there are no restrictions about running around in it either.

SHARING THE SAME TENT

Personal hygiene, yours or someone else's, can become an issue if you are sharing a tent with another pilgrim. It is not quite as fun reveling in another's dirt as it is your own. For instance, if your fellow pilgrim's feet stink as badly as my brother Micah's did during a pilgrimage through Scotland and Ireland, **force him to keep his feet in his sleeping bag with clean socks on**.

If this doesn't help or if he has no socks (Micah didn't even bring *shoes* on this pilgrimage, opting for sandals), he must clean his feet. If his feet will not unstink or if he refuses, sleep outside. If it's raining, you are in real trouble.

WHEN YOU CAN'T FIND A BATHROOM

It happens on every pilgrimage: you have to go, but there's no place to go. Here's what you do.

1. If you are in civilization (i.e., big city or small town), there is probably a Starbucks or some equivalent. Most restaurants and coffee shops have bathrooms you can use without buying anything.
2. Most hotels have a lobby bathroom. Walk in fast, before anyone can stop you, and just act like you're a guest there.
3. Find a park, any park, and look for a secluded place. Yeah, it's a bit gross, but it happens to the best of us. Always keep a few Kleenexes in your pilgrim supplies. The small, rectangular "pocket packs" travel well.
4. Don't panic. There must be someplace nearby where you can squat. Don't worry about doing it all at once. Just get the initial

business over with and do it quick. One motion. Chances are no one will notice. Do the rest later.

We were out in the wilds of southern Idaho on our way to Spokane, and for some reason Clint refused to squat in the cornfield. I don't know why. So we went from farmhouse to farmhouse asking to use the bathroom. One guy told us there were a million acres out there just waiting to help us out. He was right. Another woman finally let Clint do his business. I still cringe when I think about the damp stench radiating from her bathroom. Unless the cornfield is mined, squat.

In Boston Common, it got ugly, but I was quick!

SHAVING WITH A LEATHERMAN

Don't! You *want* to look grizzly and unkempt! It's a pilgrimage, damn it! And shaving with a Leatherman is just a plain bad idea.

Jared enjoys his road trip pilgrim grizz.

Pilgrim Cuisine and the Art of Finding Free Food

SERENITY IN CANYON DE CHELLY

My welcoming Navajo host Winnie Many Horses puts her hand on my shoulder and whispers, "Behave as you would in your white man's church."

Participation in a sweat lodge ceremony is not something to be taken casually. The experience can last up to four hours, and temperatures inside the lodge soar above 100°F. Going to church seems a lot easier.

© Photo by Martin Hartley

It is a hot July afternoon, and I have come to Arizona's Canyon de Chelly to sweat with Winnie and four of her relatives. Standing against the canyon wall, the lodge is a dome made of willow twigs covered with canvas and topped with red Arizona earth. The opening faces east to greet the dawn.

A log fire blazes a few feet away. Winnie's granddaughters toss in volcanic rocks from the nearby Chuska Mountains. When they glow red, Winnie signals me to take the pitchfork and lay them in the pit inside. She strips off her clothes and crawls into the lodge, sitting alone until the temperature is right before calling us in for the first of four sessions that will honor the spirits of earth, air, and water—the spiritual boundaries of Dinetah, or Navajo Land.

Symbolizing a return to the womb of Mother Earth and the innocence of childhood, the ceremony is meant to purify body, mind, and spirit. For the Navajo, the sweat lodge is a place of spiritual refuge and mental and physical healing, a place to get answers and guidance by asking the Creator and Mother Earth for wisdom and power.

I am the last to enter the lodge. In the sudden blackness I cannot see a thing other than the glowing red rocks, but my other senses sharpen immediately.

I smell the cedar bark we sit on and feel the obsessive heat and the touch of the sweaty shoulders of the other women pressed against me.

In her melodic Navajo tongue, Winnie begins her first song – for the Spirit of Canyon de Chelly, Spider Woman. The relatives join, and after a while I sing along with words I did not know I knew.

Between songs, the silence is broken by a raven's shriek bouncing off the canyon walls outside. Winnie sprinkles sage and cedar needles on the red rocks, followed by water. My breath instantly goes shallow from the searing steam, but I start to relax as I inhale the sweet smell of cedar. Winnie gathers her strength for the last song of this session. Afterward, the blanket over the doorway flaps up like an eyelid and we crawl out, dripping and exposed, into the hot bright air.

We take refuge under a shady piñon tree. The sun feels dry and hostile. I rub sage all over my body, which is rejuvenating. Later we burrow back into the sweat lodge for three more sessions. Winnie blesses me so that no harm will befall me while traveling home. At the end of the final session, she remains behind.

"She is singing a prayer of thanks to the spirits of Canyon de Chelly," explains a granddaughter.

We have a final sage bath, dress, and stroll away arm-in-arm as sisters.

— *Bernice Notenboom, writer, adventurer, and owner of* Moki Treks (www.mokitreks.com)

Just as there is a certain art to finding accommodations, so there is an art to eating on your journey. No five-star-restaurant suggestions here, just some thoughts on how to eat cheaply or even for free. As with all aspects of the journey, it also requires a shift in perspective: Instead of thinking of yourself as deprived as you eat your tenth peanut butter sandwich in three days, think of it as a challenge, a spiritual and culinary path toward pilgrim enlightenment. And after a while, you might even enjoy that sandwich . . . maybe.

THE CELEBRATORY FEAST

No matter how impoverished you may be on your road trip pilgrimage, always keep a hidden stash for the all-important "Celebratory Feast." Milestones along the course of the journey, like arriving at the ocean for the first time, must be properly celebrated!

HAUTE CUISINE, PILGRIM-STYLE

Something magical happens when you're on the road: everything tastes better. A bland meal of noodles and rice becomes kingly fare. And even eating the same stuff over and over has a certain charm. Here are a few dishes that have become pilgrim staples for me and my pals through the years.

THE MIRACLE OF PEANUT BUTTER SANDWICHES

It may not sound appetizing, but we ate peanut butter sandwiches as often as six times a day while biking across America. They're cheap, provide lots of energy and protein, and store easily. A few tips for transit, however:

1. Do not store extra sandwich bread next to the camp stove. Your bread will smell like gas. For weeks we wondered why our bread smelled funny and why we felt a little woozy after lunch.
2. Chunky or creamy peanut butter, it doesn't matter. Though there are some pilgrims who contest that chunky is more masculine (I'm sort of a closet-creamy guy myself).
3. Honey and jam travel pretty well. You'll find plenty of free samples at most diners and fast-food restaurants.

THE JOYS OF SLUDGE

Cheap, easy, and tasty, sludge is the great pasta/soup packet delicacy. All you do is dump a few Lipton noodle-soup packets in a pot with a whole ton of pasta and rice, boil off the water, and enjoy. We thought we were really onto something clever until an English pilgrim in Yellowstone took a taste and confided: "Seems everybody who goes on a journey has a variation of this stuff, don't you think?" Hmmm, so much for originality. Here are some of our variations.

YELLOWSTONE SLUDGE

Same recipe as standard sludge. Just add a couple of instant macaroni-and-cheese packets to give it that golden color.

SHAKESPEAREAN SLUDGE

We ate this crunchy sludge during a visit to Stratford-upon-Avon. Follow the directions for standard sludge, but add three unwashed carrots and potatoes. The sludge will not only cook the potatoes, but clean them too! (Micah came up with this sludge recipe; it has not been repeated since.)

SLUDGE NICOISE

Add tuna fish, hardboiled eggs, olives, capers, anchovies, and a dash of red wine vinegar to the classic sludge recipe. Yum! And *very* healthy.

FIVE TASTY, SIMPLE MEALS FOR UNDER A BUCK

1. Peanut butter sandwich. Cost: about forty cents per sandwich.
2. Sludge. Cost: about a buck per batch per pilgrim, including camp-stove fuel.
3. Cheap veggie stew. Buy the cheapest veggies in the store, whatever they are: cabbage, leeks, parsnips, etc. Throw them into the pot with any leftovers. (One time in England we bought a cabbage, popped it into the pot whole, boiled it up, and that was dinner.) Cost: less than a buck per pilgrim, including camp-stove fuel.
4. Tuna fish sandwich. Cost: about eighty cents per sandwich.
5. Ash cakes. Make bread dough out of flour and water. Throw on warm campfire ashes. Cost: about three cents per ash cake. (My brother Micah has become the master ash-cake baker.)

SCORING FREE EATS

Throughout the course of many pilgrimages, we've become quite adept at getting free food. A buck saved here, a buck there—it really adds up. A free lunch or dinner now and then is a huge shot in the arm to the pilgrim's treasury (a communal Altoids tin, full of change and bills, during a bike trip through Scotland with my brothers, for instance). Here are some ideas for eating free on a pilgrimage.

GETTING INVITED OVER FOR BREAKFAST, LUNCH, OR DINNER

1. Camp out in a visible spot. Locals will get curious and come chat.
2. Stay in a place for a few days. People will start to know you and you'll get dinner invitations.
3. Camp out right across the street from some nice, tidy, unassuming houses. Then sleep in. In the morning the folks across the street will see you sprawled out near their front yard and invite you over.

4. Attend local events such as weddings, bar mitzvahs, church dinners, and birthday parties. Mix and mingle. You may think at first that people will scorn your impromptu visit. And they may. But never fear, once they find out you're pilgrims, you'll be the guests of honor. (Just remember to be cordial, gracious, charming, and, you guessed it, tell many great stories from your adventures.)

GETTING LEFTOVERS FROM RESTAURANTS

Follow the steps below for a relatively surefire method of dining out for free.

1. Roll in late, like right before the restaurant is about to close.
2. Make friends with the waitresses. They'll ask you about the journey. Impress them with your courage and sensitivity.
3. Order something small, like bread. They'll ask you if that is all you want. You say, "Yes." Then they'll say, "But you must be hungry from pilgrimaging." And you'll respond, "Yes, but this is all we can afford." They will bring you all the leftovers they can find.

While biking across America, we rolled into the Glen Ferris Inn in West Virginia, ten minutes before closing. The waitresses were sexy and the food was terrific. We even took away doggie bags for breakfast! And better yet, if you're making a movie about the quest, tell the manager or owner you'll put them in the credits of the film if they give you free food. This approach has worked wonders from Sawtooth City, Idaho, to Kompong Cham, Cambodia. Everybody loves free publicity.

RULES OF ETIQUETTE FOR BARGING IN ON COMMUNITY FEASTS

1. When you find a community feast, let the locals invite you to feast with them. This makes for enhanced camaraderie and a greater possibility of leftovers. We came across a community breakfast in Ashton, Wyoming, as part of the town's Fourth of July celebrations and were immediately invited to the table. A kind organic farmer even invited us over to his place for a lunch of fresh-grown salad greens.

2. Tell many great stories from your adventure. You have to pay for your meal somehow.
3. Compliment the chefs on the food. Tell them how you've eaten nothing but peanut butter sandwiches and sludge for weeks (true). They will be thrilled to save you from your culinary wasteland and probably send you on your way with leftovers.

WHEN BARGING IN ON CHURCH DINNERS . . .

Follow the same rules as above and be courteous if you get goaded into attending services. Try your hand at singing hymns. It might be fun!

A FEW MORE SUGGESTIONS FOR SCORING FREE OR SUPER CHEAP SNACKS ON THE ROAD

1. **Wineries.** Most wineries have tasting hours. Nothing on earth beats a little Pinot Noir, cheese, and crackers on a pilgrimage.
2. **Orchards.** Sneak in and make off with some fruit. Or, stop in at the roadside stand (many orchards have one) and befriend the orchard keeper.
3. **Farmer's markets.** Farmers love pilgrims. They'll often give you free or very inexpensive eats. Two melon farmers in Kentucky loaded up the Ark of the Covenant with free honeydews during our trip across America.
4. **Roadside beef-jerky stands** (usually run out of the back of somebody's pickup). Find these all over the Western United States. The jerky is often homemade and the folks running the stands are laid-back and generous.

THE CALCULUS OF CONDIMENTS

You can easily find free ketchup, mustard, honey, jam, salt, and pepper at most fast-food places. Keep a running supply of plastic pouches in your backpack or bike trailer. Look how much money it can save over the course of a three-month pilgrimage for three pilgrims:

Ketchup:	6 bottles @ $2.50/bottle =	$15.00
Honey:	6 jars @ $4.00/jar =	$24.00
Mustard:	2 jars @ $3.00/jar =	$6.00
Salt/Pepper:	2 shakers@ $1.50/shaker =	$3.00
Jam:	8 jars @ $4.00/jar =	$32.00
	Total = $80.00	

OK, so it ain't gonna cover that penthouse suite at the Bellagio, but on a pilgrimage, every little bit counts.

WORKING ON THE ROAD

If all else fails and you just need to make some money, getting a job on the road is always an option. Not only will it supply you with some quick cash, but it can often be a fulfilling diversion, allowing you to meet some locals. Since diving into local life is what a pilgrimage is all about, running out of money and having to pick up a job for a few days is actually a blessing. There is no better way to immerse yourself in humanity than to work alongside another human being. And those hours spent simply working do wonders for clearing the head and making your life come into focus. In some ways, work can be as edifying as any other element of the journey.

We rolled into Nauvoo, Illinois, on a damp night in July, completely broke. We dropped by a community gathering and, naturally, people came up to ask us what we were doing. I told them we were looking for a job. We were working by noon the next day hauling hotel furniture around. I've talked to other road trip pilgrims who've picked up random jobs on farms, in orchards, in shops, in sawmills, in hotels, and on ranches for days, weeks, or even months to fund the rest of their journeys.

Remember, people will want to encourage your quest as most are enormously inspired by someone pursing their dreams.

Here are some ways to find work on the road.

1. Find a nice small- to medium-sized town that has a healthy, active feel. Choose a town with a decent economy. Beware of boarded-up storefronts and tossed classifieds. An agricultural town can be

good too, as farmers often hire extra help during the harvest. The same is true of vineyards during the crush as well as orchards in the fall.

2. Read *The Grapes of Wrath.* No matter how hard up you may be, somebody else has it worse and needs a job more. It will help you appreciate the job you do get.

3. Go to a community event, a farmer's market, a baseball game, whatever. Talk to everyone you can, tell them you're on an epic journey (to Walden Pond, Samarqand, the birthplace of Gandhi, etc.), and that you just ran out of money and would like to work. Somebody will know someone who needs some extra work done for a few days.

"Nothing ever comes to one, that is worth having, except as a result of hard work."
— *Booker T. Washington*

CHAPTER 6

Mythological Monsters and Other Perils

WALKING BERMUDA

"I have always believed that the best way to see a place is by foot. Walking or hiking allows you to become intimately in touch with your direction, the ground you've covered; there is no barrier

between you and your natural surroundings. With nothing but your shoes and your backpack, you are solely committed to the journey, relying on your own strength to carry you onward.

"That's how I came up with the idea to walk across Bermuda, a twenty-one-square-mile archipelago of more than one hundred islands in the Atlantic Ocean, hundreds of miles away from the nearest continent. We would walk twenty-six miles, from east to west, across the islands and over the bridges and causeways that connect them, all in one day. In August, my friend Courtney and I set out early from the town of St. Georges, the oldest British colony in existence. And in the ten and a half hours that it took us to complete the trek, we discovered breathtaking views, unknown trails, wild goats, secluded beaches, seventeenth-century architecture, and five centuries of history. Most importantly, we discovered a new perspective on an island we thought we knew. We discovered we had the determination to make a goal and achieve it, to push ourselves and our bodies in a way we had never done.

The end of the journey brought a complicated yet poignant happiness. The trip we had so anticipated was over, the question of 'could we do it' was answered, and we would never experience it for the first time again. But, in a small way, we had transformed ourselves in the process.

"I used to imagine glorious, exotic adventures to secluded reaches of the globe, but what I realized was, adventure is always within reach. Every place has its own exotic allure. In length it was a small pilgrimage, but it had a huge impact on my life. It will always stand out as my first authentic journey, the one that started it all."

— *Brittany Myers, marketing coordinator,*
New York City

You've been on the road for a while. Despite the amazing kindness of those around you, all pilgrims must battle their share of monsters; it is a rite of passage, like Hercules and his twelve labors. Here are a few monsters and other perils you may encounter on your pilgrimage.

WEATHER

You're certain to encounter everything from dust storms to monsoons if you pilgrimage long enough and far enough. Experiencing a range of weather (sun and rain, mist and sleet) gives the pilgrimage a necessary texture. Sunshine all the time is nice for a vacation, but for a pilgrimage, embrace whatever weather you receive.

RAIN

Depending on when and where you take your pilgrimage, you may encounter a few days or weeks of rain. Here's how to deal.

1. You must embrace the rain, not just put up with it or try to forget about it. You must make it your friend. Trying to stay dry will just exacerbate the problem. As a society we tend to see rain as "bad weather" and anything sunny as "good weather." But a road trip pilgrimage is all about stripping away those constructs. Biking in the rain can be meditative and helps you lose yourself to the road. Sunshine all the time can get monotonous. Mist in the morning is atmospheric, magical. Every type of weather can be a blessing on a pilgrimage if you choose to see it that way.

2. Make up clever songs about the rain. It will help to lighten the situation.

Drying out after a big storm in Nebraska

3. Admit you have no control over the rain, and therefore, you are going to gain control by not caring if it rains for a month straight. And it might!

4. Bring along plenty of plastic bags and wrap up everything, like clothes and sleeping bags. It's much easier to enjoy being wet if you know you have a warm sleeping bag and dry clothes waiting. Ironically, nothing works quite as well at keeping clothes and other things dry as cheap (or free), heavy-duty plastic bags.

HEADWINDS

When pilgrimaging by bike especially, the three most feared natural obstacles are heat (and humidity), hills, and headwinds, with headwinds taking the cake. You can outlast or get used to the heat (or bike at night when it's cooler), you can grind to the top of the hill knowing you will enjoy racing down the other side, but for headwinds, there is no payoff. You just have to deal with them and here's how.

1. Take a break until the winds pass.
2. Bike at night when winds generally die down.
3. See it as an endurance challenge, relishing the pain and the toning of your calves.

Jared battles headwinds in Scotland.

The headwinds got so bad along the Gulf Coast of Mexico that I pushed my bike on flat ground for miles. The winds lasted three days, but died down at night.

Facing brutal headwinds while biking up to Spokane along the Salmon River, Clint finally had all he could take. He ducked his head and rode as hard as he could in a furious attempt to "beat" the headwinds. You can imagine who won (this strategy is not recommended).

MUD AND SPRINKLERS

Mud and sprinklers may sound innocuous, but don't be fooled! They top my list of road trip–pilgrim deterrents.

MUD

You may camp in a field of dirt, only to wake up the next morning in a field of muck. Rain will do that; it happened to me in Mexico. This is what you do.

1. Find the humor in it. Take pictures to show the folks back home.
2. See how much muck you can accumulate on the bottoms of your shoes or sandals.
3. Clean off your tent and other stuff later. It's a losing battle now. Be one with the mud until you have an opportunity to clean it off for good (or at least for a while).

My sneaks were never the same after messing with that muddy field in Mexico.

SPRINKLERS

Sprinklers are the bane of the pilgrim, ruining otherwise peaceful camp-sites at parks, picnic areas, and churchyards with their mutinous and un-expected blasts of water in the middle of the night. There are three main types: classic Rain Birds, mushrooms, and roboheads. The latter are by far the most dangerous. Check out the descriptions and accompanying illustration below for how to disarm each kind of sprinkler and secure your camp. It'll save you countless nights of lost sleep.

CLASSIC RAIN BIRDS

Classic Rain Birds are identified by their chicken-shaped head and clas-sic *cha-cha-cha* sound. They are easily disarmed with a bungee cord. Just wrap the bungee around the neck of the sprinkler and it will shoot off all night long in one direction.

MUSHROOMS

These sprinklers are easily identified by their distinct mushroom shape. Do not be fooled by their harmless appearance! The mushroom can strike at anytime! Fortunately, once it does strike, the mushroom, like the classic Rain Bird, is easily disarmed by wrapping a bungee cord around its neck.

Mushroom sprinkler sitting quietly in fresh-laid sod in Colorado

ROBOHEADS

The most feared of all sprinklers, roboheads are identified by their round, small head, lurking below the surface of the grass, preparing for the right moment to spring. Ro-boheads are difficult to detect at night and, when they pop up, cast a razor-thin, razor-sharp stream of water through the air. They cannot be disarmed with bungee cords. Hauling a steel garbage can on top of them or covering them with

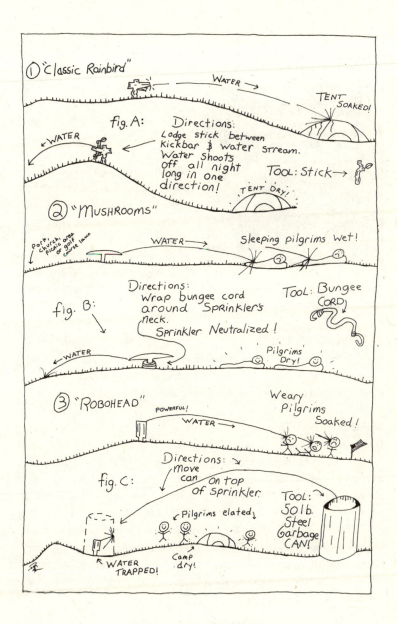

your sludge pot and anchoring it down with tent stakes and bungee cords is your best bet.

Whoever authored this sign, at a roadside park in Parachute, Colorado, is no doubt aware of the threat sprinklers pose to road trip pilgrims. I found it quite alarming that they would use this cowardly and shameful intimidation method as a way to deter pilgrims. Fortunately, this park is equipped with easily defused mushroom sprinklers. Use the information above to disarm them with bungee cords and don't let these idle threats keep you from your well-deserved slumber!

MAN AND BEAST

Perhaps even more dangerous than sprinklers, the perils posed by everything from desert hermits to vicious hounds have assailed pilgrims for millennia. Here is how to stay alive and continue the quest.

DESERT HERMITS

Desert hermits have chosen to live where they do for several possible reasons: insanity, intense dislike of people, and/or love of the desert and its requisite solitude. So be careful not to cross the hermit. It is easy to do, as the hermit sees his territory as *terra sagrada* and any slight, no matter how unintentional, may cause him to snap.

Jared, Clint, and I crossed a desert hermit in Amboy, California, during our bike trip across America. This guy claimed to own the whole town, even the post office. Late that night, we camped way off the side of the road in the middle of nowhere and listened as his henchmen came trawling by in the darkness, looking for us.

Disclaimer: This is actually not a desert hermit; it's my Uncle Gary. But he looks a lot like a desert hermit, don't you think? And he actually has a lot of experience as a mountain hermit (albeit a very kind and generous one).

If you cross a desert hermit, this is what you do.

1. Leave town as soon as possible. If it's too hot to ride, wait until it cools down and then split.
2. Set up camp where he is not likely to find you, way off the side of the road, out of range of headlights.
3. Don't underestimate the desert hermit's propensity for payback. After all, he's got nothing else to do.

BELLIGERENT DRUNKS

Pilgrims are a curiosity. They attract all sorts, including belligerent drunks looking for someone to harass.

If accosted on bike or foot by a belligerent drunk, do the following:

1. Stay calm. Hasty action will only escalate the situation.

2. Pretend you don't understand what they want. Playing dumb can be a good strategy for everything from dealing with drunks to getting across the border.

3. Buy time until another car or person comes along. Then make a break for it.

Holidays in many foreign countries, as well as the United States, can be a great time to pilgrimage, but a bad time to do so late at night. Late one Christmas Eve in Champoton, Mexico, two drunk guys accosted me after midnight Mass. They grabbed my mountain bike and demanded drug money. I played it cool until another car rolled up to the intersection, then made a break for it. If they've got a weapon or if the situation escalates, however, just fork over your wallet. It's much better than a gunshot wound.

THE POSER PILGRIM

Just like anything, there are the **true pilgrims,** folks who are on the road for the love of it, just minding their own business, soaking up life, and seeking their shrine, and then there are the **poser pilgrims,** who leech off their fellow pilgrims, think they know everything, and can't stand running into pilgrims who don't care about their exploits. Signs you're dealing with a poser pilgrim:

1. Will attempt to wow you with his wisdom, his pilgrim acumen, and his adventure stories.

2. Will tell you everything you are doing wrong, which, conveniently, he is doing right.

3. Will attempt to convince you that his is the only way to go on a journey.

4. May try to steal your food.

5. May try to frighten you about what dangers lie ahead.

6. Has no magical tokens.

A poser pilgrim on a bike lectured us in Nebraska during our journey across America. He found it absurd that we didn't use clipless pedals. After his lengthy diatribe, he attempted to dismount his bike, but his pedal wouldn't disengage. I won't soon forget the valiant struggle he made to stay standing, but ended up on the ground anyway with a horrible crash. Given time, the poser pilgrim will always undo himself.

In Northern Ireland a poser pilgrim attempted to wow us with all the newspaper articles he'd weaseled his way into. He even tried to guilt-trip us into giving him one of our camp mats for the night, claiming all he'd brought with him on his adventure for sleeping arrangements was a hammock. A hammock? Are you out of your mind? You're biking through Northern Ireland, pal, not the Amazon. I love hammocks as much as the next guy, but honestly.

Do not be manipulated by a poser pilgrim! Their game is preying upon the goodwill of fellow pilgrims for things they could easily take care of themselves. Remember: *It is your pilgrimage*. Take care to have the journey you want and don't let any poser pilgrim screw it up.

THE CAMP HOST AND HIS WILY DOG

We've already talked about camp hosts, those crafty old folks who run the campgrounds and make it difficult for pilgrims to get away with a free snooze. All camp hosts have a little sidekick: a yappy, annoying poodle-type dog. These dogs typically answer to names such as Snookims, Cuddly, or Fluffy. Don't let their innocuous names fool you! They may be no more than ten pounds, but their size in no way corresponds to the amount of noise they can make. If you set them off, they'll never stop barking. And if they get off their chain, they will tail you through the campground until you're caught. To avoid the camp host and his dog:

1. Roll in late to the campground.
2. Go into stealth mode as you creep past the camp-host site, taking care not to wake the monster. Most camp-host sites are located at the entrance to the campground. If you suspect the camp host or his dog is still prowling about, scope out the area first and find a clever way to get in without being seen, such as tromping through the woods to get to the campground instead of using the main entrance.

Nothing cute about this pilgrim-hating camp-host sidekick

VICIOUS HOUNDS

All pilgrims have encounters with these monsters, especially in rural areas. And dogs in developing countries pose a real threat as potential carriers of rabies. When tailed by a vicious hound, this is what you do. If you're on foot . . .

1. Back away slowly from the hound.
2. Use your backpack as a shield.
3. If necessary, bribe the hound with leftover PB and J.
4. Command the hound to GO BACK! Remember, you are a pilgrim. You have authority over such creatures (or at least you can try to sound like you do).

If you're on a bike . . .

See if you can outrun the hound.

If you can't outrun it . . .

1. Have one of your fellow pilgrims cause a distraction. Confuse the hound.

2. If you have a bike trailer, swerve from side to side in an attempt to sideswipe the hound as he pursues. Be careful not to wreck; this is an expert-only maneuver.

3. If you get to the top of a hill, make a break for it. You will probably be able to outrun the hound going downhill.

4. Try throwing a stick or something. Sometimes these beasts are distracted by a game of fetch. (They may tag along for miles, however.)

5. Command the hound to GO BACK! (like above). Late one night in northern Idaho, we were riding through a rural township when suddenly a vicious dog leapt snarling out of the shadows. I turned and yelled at it to GO BACK! The dog ran away whimpering. True story.

Or, just rub the hound's furry belly. Vicious hounds are like anything else; they just need a little love.

ADVENTURER VERSUS CERBERUS

According to my MD brother Jared: "Dogs remain a significant threat to the adventurer regardless of what continent (with the exception of Antarctica, but I hear those penguins can be pretty aggressive). In the United States alone there are estimated to be more than 4.7 million dog bites per year. About 800,000 of these result in a visit to a physician. The most vicious breeds are pit bulls, rottweilers, malamutes, husky types, wolf hybrids, German shepherds, and mixed breeds (aka mutts).

"Here are a few simple guidelines for dog-bite prevention and treatment.

"**Don't run.** Nothing provokes the biting instinct in a dog like feeling he's a wolf again, running down a helpless fawn. So the first principle is that if a dog attacks you, don't run.

"**Hold your ground.** Stand with your legs together, arms over your chest, with your fists covering your neck.

"If you're knocked to the ground, **lie still in a fetal position,** with knees brought up to the chest, fists over the back of the neck, and forearms covering your ears. If you lie still long enough, the dog will lose interest and go away. It's not a masculine pose, but it may save you a costly trip to the plastic surgeon.

"If you're on a bike and get attacked, either **pedal like hell or stop abruptly** and use your bike as a shield from the dog. In our experience, pedaling like hell has had great success. Most dogs can't run as fast as a bike for very long and most dogs will quit after a few hundred yards.

"**Dogs love to bite**. If you do get bitten, here's what you should do.

"**Don't panic.** This happens all the time to lots of people, and most end up doing just fine.

"**Wash the area thoroughly** with copious amounts of clean

water. Ten to fifteen minutes of constant irrigation may be necessary to fully cleanse the area. If you have alcohol or Betadine, these can also be used to disinfect the area, but clean water is usually sufficient.

"Do I need antibiotics? Anywhere from 5 to 20 percent of dog bites get infected, so most physicians would recommend taking prophylactic antibiotics after a bite.

"The most common organisms are Pasteurella multocida and Staphylococcus aureus. Amoxicillin-clavulanic acid (Augmentin) is the drug of choice for dealing with these two types of infection. If you have a penicillin allergy, then doxycycline is a good alternative.

"You should take antibiotics for three to seven days if there is no sign of infection. If there are signs of infection, then you should take antibiotics for ten to fourteen days.

"*Remember:* If the redness, swelling, pain, or drainage gets worse, even while taking antibiotics, you should be seen by a physician immediately, as this may indicate a more serious infection.

"Do I need a tetanus shot? No, if you have had one in the last ten years and the bite was relatively clean. If the wound was contaminated with feces or soil, then you should get a tetanus booster if you haven't had one in the past five years.

"Do I need a rabies vaccine? Fortunately, in the United States, rabies is rarely acquired from dogs; the top transmitters are raccoons, skunks, and bats. Still, cases are reported from time to time, and erring on the side of caution is warranted, as rabies is a universally fatal disease. Unfortunately, rabies remains common in the canine population in developing countries, especially among mangy strays.

"A bite from an unprovoked dog is more likely to cause rabies than one from a provoked dog.

"Try to find the owner of the offending dog. They should

be able to provide evidence of rabies vaccination. If the dog has been vaccinated, then you don't need to worry about rabies.

"If you can't find the owner or if there is uncertainty about the dog's vaccination status, then just assume it hasn't been vaccinated.

"If bitten by an unvaccinated dog, then you need to be seen by a physician and given rabies immunoglobulin and rabies vaccine by intramuscular injection. These treatments should be started within forty-eight hours of the bite.

"Additional information about dog bites, rabies, and other travel-related medical concerns can be found at the Center for Disease Control (CDC) website: *www.cdc.gov*."

—*Jared Austin, M.D.*

BUNNIES

Yeah, you think they're cute, but as I mentioned earlier, bunnies (especially en masse) can be creepy. We biked through this bizarre valley overrun with cottontails in Scotland. It was an epidemic! Bunnies were so plentiful we had to swerve to dodge them as they streaked by the dozens across the road; the hillsides were honeycombed with their burrows. Terrifying! All the farmhouses in this cursed valley were empty, gutted, abandoned. The bunnies had driven everybody out. We heard a telltale gunshot at one point, the only sign of life, and saw, far across the bunny-strewn fields, a lone Scot with a shotgun, walking and shooting, walking and shooting. "Bunny stew again tonight, hon. Yummy!"

TRICKY VARMINTS

When you hit a touristy area on your pilgrimage, you'll likely encounter tricky varmints that have learned to subsist by preying upon unsuspecting pilgrims. These varmints may be the macaques of Angkor Wat in Cambodia, the pillaging seagulls of Venice Beach, the squirrels of Mammoth Hot Springs in Yellowstone, or worst of all, the wily coatis of Iguazú Falls.

Walking down a path near Iguazú Falls in Brazil, lunch swinging from my hand, minding my own business, a cute little coati (a sort of snouty raccoon) waddled over and placed his paws on the bag and stared up at me with these huge, trusting, vulnerable eyes. How cute, I thought. Then one of his buddies came over. Then another buddy and then another. And suddenly the first coati jumped on the bag and another clawed up my leg, then two more coatis jumped on the first coati!

Yeah, try telling that to ten ferocious coatis.

Terrified, I tossed the bag as far as I could and *ten* coatis pounced. Where did they all come from? They tore the plastic bag to shreds, biting and snarling with ferocious abandon! All the other tourists stopped to watch and laugh. The Brazilian girl who'd somehow attached herself to me pointed to a "Do not feed the animals" sign. I know, I know, silly American thinking the varmints just wanted a belly rub.

To successfully get mugged by these wily critters, do the following:

1. Walk down a forest path in a tropical, touristy area where varmints beg for free eats.
2. Your lunch should be in a plastic bag with the lunchmeat already open, hanging from your hand.
3. When a varmint comes to smell the bag, believe that the varmint is just saying hi, and has no ulterior motives.
4. Toss your lunch to keep from being torn apart by varmints.

MOSQUITOES AND MIDGES

Mosquitoes and biting midges (a subgroup of gnats) may be the worst scourge of all, but like everything, they have their kryptonite. These bugs don't like campfire smoke. Huddle around a fire made with wet bark and wood. It may help to saturate your clothes with the smoke, too. Also,

carry insect repellent with a high (at least 30 percent) DEET content. And beware in tropical regions where mosquitoes may carry malaria. In these climes use DEET, cover up, drag along a mosquito net for sleeping, and, if you're so inclined, get a prescription for Doxycycline, Malarone, or another malaria prophylaxis before you go. Steer clear of the malaria drug Lariam as the nightmares are just not worth it.

MONTEZUMA'S REVENGE

I don't think I have ever been on a long pilgrimage in a developing country and not gotten some sort of stomach sickness (though usually mild). It's simply your body adjusting to life on the road in a totally new place: new food, new bugs, new everything. This is how to deal.

View the sickness as a ritual purification, a necessary rite of passage for the pilgrimage.

If this doesn't work . . .

View the sickness as a sign that great pilgrim bounty lies ahead, if you can only stick it out.

If this doesn't work . . .

You know the drill. Rest up and push the fluids.

Jared and I both got nasty diarrhea on the Inca trail in Peru. I don't think it really enhanced anything, but it was sort of a humorous bonding experience.*

HUMOROUS BONDING EXPERIENCES

They're really what pilgrimages are all about. The most arduous experiences for the road trip pilgrim are often the things you reflect back upon most fondly. Try and see all obstacles from a dual perspective, one firmly grounded in the moment and the other looking back from a future time when, yeah, this is actually going to be funny. Remember, there is no greater satisfaction than having *lived* a good story.

CHAPTER 7

Physical Rigors of the Quest

TALE OF THE TOUR

"I met Marta in third grade and Megan in sixth, and the three of us were inseparable until we graduated from high school. We went off to different colleges and different lives, but we have always stayed close. These days, living in separate cities, we like to get together every few years. We've been avid Tour de France fans since the nineties, so we landed on the idea of going to see the race. Before I knew it, the three of us had purchased plane tickets, rented bikes in France, and had euros in hand. We would cycle in the Pyrenees for a week, then head to Slovenia to visit my family's homeland.

"Our most exciting day attending the tour was stage 15, which took the racers 207 kilometers over six major climbs. We cycled the Col de Peyresourde that day, which was a Category I climb in the day's route. Let me translate that: Peyresourde, a thirteen-kilometer climb with average gradient 6.9 percent, was classified by the tour organizers in the second-hardest category of climbs. Let me translate that again: riding the Col *hurt*. A lot. It took us most of the morning to reach the top. The pro riders would make the climb later in the day in what seemed like minutes.

"As we rode, my lungs and quads were burning, but I don't think I've ever been happier. The atmosphere was incredible, like being at the best outdoor concert of all time. People camp for days along the route to get the best vantage spots for the tour, and these very same spectators cheer you on as though you, too, are a tour participant. *"Allez! Allez!"* they root for you. You get a flat? Simply hop off your bike, and someone runs over to fix it, like having your very own pit crew. Language barriers were nonexistent that day, because everyone can smile. Once the tour caravan went by, we rode back to our bed-and-breakfast and watched the end of the stage with some fifty other sweaty, rabid tour fans from all over the world. The sense of community was unreal.

"Perhaps my favorite interaction of the day was with a fellow rider. I'm a college professor and I had a ball cap from my school (Washington and Jefferson College) attached to the back of my pack. As I plodded up the Col, I was able to pass some other riders, but more often, I was getting passed. One man with a Scottish accent encouraged me as he blew by: 'C'mon, lassie! Do the presidents proud!'

"Cycling commentator Bob Roll says that attending the tour will change your life. He's right. That day on the Col de Peyresourde was unbelievable, and it was only the second day of the trip. I could easily write volumes about the wonderful experiences I had in France and Slovenia. And I learned a lot of surprising things. French croissants fuel you better than Powerade. You really can survive for two weeks on thirty-three pounds of luggage sans blow dryer. Lonely Planet language guides are good for all kinds of pickup lines but omit handy phrases like "Where the hell is my luggage?" Ultimately, though, the experience highlighted for me an essential paradox of pilgrimage: it is best undertaken alone *and* with lifelong friends. It is best to dive into the unexpected and to delve into your past in the exact same moment.

"Between Marta, Megan, and me, there was about ninety years of friendship up on that mountain. We are currently planning our next trip, to Charleston, South Carolina, for a long weekend. We can't manage two weeks in Europe every year, but every year can be about investing in these friendships and adding a few more pages to that well-worn diary."

— *Jenny Kline, college professor,*
Washington, Pennsylvania

© Photo by Marla Aufmuth

As if facing mythological monsters and dealing with midges wasn't enough . . . the quest makes many physical demands on the road trip pilgrim. Like everything on a pilgrimage, they will ultimately serve to enhance the journey, giving you immense satisfaction and great stories to tell when you get home.

HIGH PASSES

No pilgrimage is complete without the challenge of a mountain pass! Even though you may have to walk your gear-laden mountain bike or haul your fifty-pound backpack for hours up the dirt track or slope, it will only enhance your elation when you reach the top.

If crossing a high pass is part of your itinerary, make sure that you . . .

1. Spend a long time on top relishing the climb. You worked hard to get there; now take it easy and enjoy the view.
2. Take lots of pictures flexing next to the summit sign. Do not underestimate the importance of pictures that show you flexing by the summit sign! Get lots of shots to impress the folks back home. Not only is it fun, it will serve as a reminder of what great shape you were in. A few years down the road you'll look at that photo and go: "Damn! I was ripped!" It will be a firm reminder that you can and should maintain

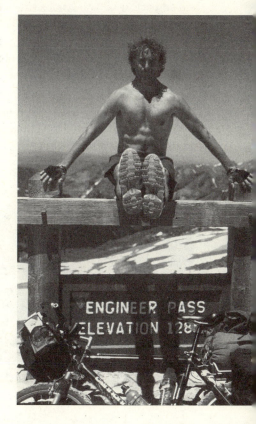

some level of fitness, enhancing your love life, your professional life, and everything else. See how one photo can change your whole destiny? (A little girl at one of my book events asked me if I "still have big muscles." I love kids.)

Terrified by the fall from grace of one of our high school heroes (who will remain nameless), Clint and I made a sacred pact to stay in shape. We call it the Oath of (insert name of fallen hero here). We ran into this onetime all-American athlete and genuine good guy years later at a wedding reception. If there was *one guy* who would *never* let himself slip, it was this guy. We didn't even recognize him at first. He just sadly stared back at us, knowing exactly what we were thinking, twisting the wedding ring around his finger and making excuses about not having a lot of time to play ball anymore . . . tragic.

So take lots of summit pictures and keep them posted in prominent locations. Somebody's looking up to you, too. You don't want to let him down.

Consult the following key for gauging the efficacy of summit-sign flex shots:

Excellent

Acceptable

Pathetic

SOME FAVORITE PASSES

Engineer Pass, Colorado. A ragged dirt road winding to a summit at more than 12,800 feet. Beautiful views and a great ride!

Forever Summit, Utah. Sweeping vista and fun dirt road.

Galena Pass, Idaho. Terrific view of the Sawtooth Mountains.

Logan Canyon Summit, Utah. Gorgeous ride and great views into Bear Lake Valley.

Forever Summit, Utah

DESERTS

There is no better place on a pilgrimage to reflect and think than in the desert. Here are a few tips for losing yourself on those magical, desolate desert highways or paths.

1. Don't eat Hershey Jumbo bars if you have no water. Clint did this in the middle of the Mojave and it was disastrous.
2. Once the sun is up, the desert heats up fast. You won't be able to sleep in, especially if you're in a tent.
3. Ride at night when the desert is serene and cool, especially on a clear, dark night with a sky full of stars.
4. Seek out a nice oasis and swim around for a while. The desert has more water than you think. Check with locals about nice swimming holes in the area. We found dozens going across the desert on various pilgrimages. These oases can become magical places, enhancing the journey both physically and spiritually.

An oasis in Arizona

DARK SPACES

Dark spaces, in our pilgrim lingo, are places where there is minimal light pollution and the sky's bounty of stars is fully visible. According to the folks at IDA (International Dark-Sky Association), it's very difficult to measure amounts of light pollution in a given area and even harder to determine places where there is zero light pollution. According to a ranger in Natural Bridges National Monument, right in the middle of the Utah desert, this far-flung no-man's-land is one of the few places in the United States where there is no light pollution and the sky attains its natural darkness. Pilgrimaging under a sea of stars is one of the great pleasures of crossing the desert.

TERRIFIC OASES IN THE DESERT

Capitol Reef National Park, Utah. The swimming hole off Route 24. Easy access and a great, quick break or pilgrim's baptism.

Just off the road in Capitol Reef National Park, Utah

Calf Creek Falls, Utah. One of the greatest swimming holes and most beautiful waterfalls in the desert, just off Route 12 near Boulder, Utah.

Round Valley, California. A hidden oasis and perfect campsite deep in the San Bernardino wilderness.

FLATLANDS

The plains get a bad rap. A lot of folks recommend crossing flatlands and "boring" agricultural areas as quickly as possible. But we've found that these places are often our favorites. Why? Perhaps it's the quiet details that inspire you: a grain silo silhouetted against the sky, a little farmhouse bracing itself for a thunderstorm, or neatly arranged rows of corn. When you really take a moment to look, the landscape will open up to you with its infinite layers.

Deep in the magic fields of Iowa

1. Don't rush; enjoy the relaxed pace. You will then be able to really appreciate the tranquil, subtle beauty of these areas.
2. Notice how everyone waves at you first. Wave back. This is friendly country.
3. See how long you can weave in and out of the dashes on the road.
4. Marvel at the wonder of creation, the gigantic fields, the epic sky, the living green . . .

BEAUTIFUL, LOW-KEY PLACES ON THE PLAINS

Ohio River between Ohio and Kentucky. We leapt back and forth across the river several times as we rode across America, finding fantastic places like Magee's in Maysville, Kentucky, a scratch bakery with their signature "salt-rising" bread. It was peaceful camping on the banks of the river, though a quick dip left me feeling a bit oily.

River Road in Northern Iowa. Pass through tidy towns along the Mississippi; at Effigy Mounds National Monument near the Minnesota border, walk the sacred ground. You can almost feel the old ghosts of these ancient Americans lingering among their burial mounds.

While enduring physical rigors, such as high passes or long stretches in the vast emptiness and terrific heat of the desert, you might wonder why you ever embarked on your pilgrimage in the first place. Those tough couple of weeks crossing the Mojave while biking across America didn't seem all that fun at the time, and yet, when reflecting back upon the trip, we relish the hot, difficult rides and endless stretches between towns almost more than anything else. Enduring physical rigors is like packing away spiritual currency. It's painful at the moment, but you can spend the interest generated for the rest of your life. I think most folks who've climbed K2 or rowed across the Atlantic or endured other truly momentous physical challenges will agree that when it's all said and done, those are the times you savor the most. It's just like posing in front of the summit sign: it's a mark of having overcome something difficult.

CHAPTER 8
Saving Graces

A PILGRIM IN HER OWN COUNTRY

"The first time I set foot in the Museum on Bendlerstrasse was in the spring of 1997 while in Berlin on a business trip. I worked for a U.S. publishing company at that time, looking after their international sales and distribution. Being German by birth, this was my prime market and so I found myself in the lucky position of becoming a pilgrim in my home country seven years after I had left it for America.

"Whether I knew a place already or not, I always made sure I set one afternoon aside to lose myself in it. This could mean visiting a particular point of interest or aimlessly promenading through a randomly chosen part of town, taking in sights, smells, and envisioning what it would feel like to live there.

"That spring of 1997 in Berlin, I had a particular point of interest: the Museum of the German Resistance dedicated to the heroes of 20 July 1944, who tragically failed in their assassination attempt on Hitler. A small group of high-profile army officers close to the Führer had risked their lives by secretly meeting over a time frame of two years to develop a carefully drafted plan which, had it been successful, would have saved millions of lives.

"But a sudden unexpected move by the dictator and the strength of a massive German oak table had prevented this course of history from happening and saved one life over millions of others, including the conspirators who were all executed by the end of the same day in the courtyard of the building that I was just about to enter now.

"Tucked away in a small tree-lined street just a few blocks away from the buzzing center of Potsdamer Platz, nothing gave away the fact that this simple building had been the heart of the German Reich's former army headquarters, the very place from which the conspirators had tried to seize power and offer surrender to the Allied Forces immediately after the bomb had gone off.

"I had been magically drawn to this place ever since finding out, almost by chance, that one of the main conspirators, General Ludwig Beck, had been an uncle of my grandmother. To celebrate a few individual heroes in the face of the massive atrocities committed by the Nazis was simply not part of a postwar German upbringing.

"Therefore, it came as no surprise when I found myself almost alone in this sparely visited memorial. Aside from me there was a class of fifth graders from England solemnly following their teacher, who pointed out handwritten letters and photographs showcased in glass cases. Also visiting was a young French couple holding hands while quietly walking through the somber rooms, as well as a few Japanese tourists, who took pictures of the brass plate that marked the wall where Ludwig Beck had found his death.

"After they moved on I stood in front of that brass plate for a long, long time. A person had died here, had died a violent death, a person who had had a father and a mother, who played as a child, who had dreams and fears, had loved, learned, ate, drank, slept, celebrated birthdays . . . and one day had died. It became clear to me that even if you have never met a person, there are many things that connect you, simply by the fact that this person is a fellow human being, related or not. And as long as we are connected in this way, human beings will care about other human beings and some will even sacrifice their lives for them.

"It was then that I realized, that while I had originally visited this place to find a piece of solace to my country's troubled past, it held a completely different message for me: Sometimes it may not be possible to console the past, but it is always possible to find hope for the future.

"Since then, every time I return to Berlin I repeat my little pilgrimage to the museum at Bendlerblock . . . until last year that is. I arrived in the capital late one night in September only to catch a very early flight back to New York the next day, spending barely ten hours in town. Unable to visit, I acknowledged my secret shrine in thought and vowed to pay tribute again next time.

"On the way to Tegel Airport in the morning, I had a lively conversation with the taxi driver, comparing one metropole to the other, when suddenly, I felt an intense shiver run down my spine. I looked up but did not recognize what I saw. 'Can you please tell me in which part of town we are right now?' I asked the driver. 'Of course!' he said. 'We just passed Bendlerblock, the former army headquarters. There is a little museum now honoring the heroes of the twentieth of July, have you ever heard of it?'"

— *Heike Bachmann, New York City*

A road trip pilgrimage is about surmounting all trials. We've already discussed the outer, physical ones (like vicious hounds, beguiling varmints, desert heat, and mountain passes), but what about the inner rigors? These can be even more challenging than the physical variety, as they tap deep into a pilgrim's soul. And yet, like the physical rigors, inner trials are essential for the spiritual progress of the pilgrim; they are, fundamentally, miracles in disguise. Without them, the pilgrim is never truly tested. As you progress through your pilgrimage, you're sure to have moments of doubt, frustration, fear, apathy, helplessness, and loneliness. Here are a few saving graces to help you turn these trials into miracles.

A PILGRIM'S BAPTISM

No matter how you are feeling on your journey, a pilgrim's baptism can instantly reinvigorate the pilgrim. Specifically, it is a leap into a lake, stream, spring, ocean, or pool (and almost always works best if the water is *cold*).

Moments after my brothers and I took a pilgrim's baptism in Grand Teton National Park, Wyoming. See how empowered we look!

1. Just find a body of water: ocean, lake, stream, whatever.
2. Charge for the water with reckless abandon.
3. Strip off most, if not all, clothes.
4. Leap into the water.
5. As you immerse yourself completely in the water, let go of all fear, all regret, all sadness, all looking back, anything that gives you pain or trouble, anything that keeps you from having the greatest journey of your life.
6. Let the water wash all the crap away.
7. Leap out of the water restored.

The journey is about looking forward, about celebrating the progression of life. It is about what will come. Leave everything else behind, just as you have left home, job, friends, stability, bed, comfort, and money behind.

Man, that was a cold one (a glacial lagoon in Iceland).

Micah takes a pilgrim's baptism in the Falls of Falloch in Scotland. (You don't have to dive unless you want to.)

A FEW MEMORABLE PILGRIM BAPTISMS

Antibes, France, 2000

Boeng Laek Lom Crater Lake, Cambodia, 2007

Chichén Itzá, Mexico, 1999

Falls of Falloch, Scotland, 2000

Hebgen Lake, Montana, 1997

Hyrum Dam, Utah, 2006

Jenny Lake, Wyoming, 2001

Jokulsalon, Iceland, 2004

Mississippi River, Illinois, 1997

Salto Cristal Falls, Paraguay, 1999

Seaside Heights, New Jersey, 1997

Venice Beach, Los Angeles, California, 1997

A pilgrim's baptism can be taken anywhere.

CLIMBING A SACRED MOUNTAIN

A pilgrim's baptism will shock you back into the present, but may still leave you longing for perspective, so climb a mountain. Every mountain can be sacred if you choose to make it so. Climb to the top and meditate on the quest. Have a little picnic, kick back, and relax. Leave anything that you feel taxing you on the summit and climb down rejuvenated.

HOLY MOUNTAINS

Just as Mount Kailash or Angkor Wat in Hindu cosmology becomes a manifestation of Mount Meru, the mythical mountain at the center of the universe, so can any mountain you climb and make sacred become your own Hero's Mountain. You may remember a shot from the summit of the Hero's Mountain in Chapter 1. The Hero's Mountain rises up a couple miles from my family's backyard in northern Utah to a summit of 8,400 feet. It was our first sacred mountain, sacred to us and maybe nobody else. Any mountain we climb, anywhere on earth, can become this mythic mountain. In the same way, any mountain you climb on your pilgrimage, if you so desire, can become sacred to you.

The rejuvenating power of climbing a sacred mountain

FAVORITE SACRED-MOUNTAIN CLIMBS

Some of these mountains are sacred to millions; some are just sacred to us.

The Hero's Mountain, Utah. Summer 1996, New Year's 1997 and 1998, summer 2007.

Croagh Patrick, Ireland. Summer 2000.

Endless steps leading down from Phnom Bokh, Cambodia

Some mountain on the Isle of Skye. Summer 2000. I don't even know its name, but it became sacred to us and revitalized our quest.

Phnom Bokh, Phnom Kulen, and Phnom Krom, Cambodia. Winter 2007. Three sacred mountains in Cambodia. Phnom Kulen is the most sacred mountain to Khmers. From its summit, King Jayavarmin the VII initiated the kingdom of Angkor in AD 800, which would last for almost four hundred years.

OVERCOMING INTERNAL DEMONS

As with physical rigors, you can see internal demons as trials or miracles. Remember, everything on a pilgrimage can be for your ultimate edification and empowerment if you allow it to be.

LOSING STUFF

What road trip pilgim hasn't lost something (maybe many things) during the course of the journey?

Never be concerned if you lose something; be concerned if you don't. If you're totally absorbed in the pilgrimage, stuff is just plain gonna get lost.

When you lose something, **don't worry about it.** You don't need it anyway.

If you lose something really important, like a passport:

See it for what it is: a great story. You'll get the problem solved and you'll have a great story to tell. And what's better than having lived a great story?

LACK OF MEANING

No matter how enthusiastically you attack your pilgrimage, if you're on the road long enough, you will probably have moments when the journey will begin to lack meaning. And the best way to deal with it is to go deeper into yourself, either through sincere interactions with your fellow pilgrims or by delving into your own thoughts. And the best way I've found to do this is to keep a journal.

Keeping a journal endows your pilgrimage with meaning, helping

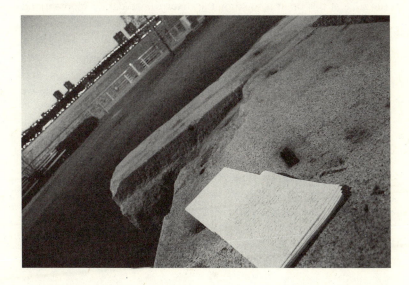

your experiences to live on, long past the completion of the quest. The process of writing down your pilgrimage enhances it. You'll remember and cherish the things you write about more than the things you don't.

1. Write every day. Make it a daily practice. Write whatever you can, even if it's just a single word.
2. Don't worry about how much you write or how sloppy your handwriting is. Just write.
3. Look back on past entries. They will enrich the journey and inform the moment.
4. Get your companions to keep journals, too. If everybody's doing it, it's easier to make time for it and to be consistent.

MONOTONY

Monotony goes hand in hand with a lack of meaning. After you've seen your fifty-seventh temple or eaten your thirtieth plate of rice and beans, it may be hard to get excited about even the most spectacular site. Even as you're progressing through your journey and the scenery is continually changing, you may have moments when it all just blends together. The trick at this point is to study the details. Ease back a moment and really *see* where you are, no matter where that is. A blasé roadside café suddenly becomes a multilayered temple of humanity. The tile on the floor, the worn chairs, the stained tablecloth—they all vibrate with the life that has happened here. Take a break, slow down, really look. And when you begin to see and feel and sense the details, the whole canvas of your pilgrimage will explode with color.

STRESS

Whether it's because you're stuck in the middle of nowhere with a broken-down bike or Jeep, or you simply feel overwhelmed by the journey, stress is another obstacle most pilgrims have to deal with.

Here are some stress-reducing techniques.

1. Get rid of the checklist. Chances are you're feeling stressed because you have too many things you're trying to do. The world's a big place and there is no limit to what you can attempt to squeeze into

a road trip pilgrimage. But remember, it's all about quality. Seeing something just because everyone else has seen it is a sure way to miss those special places along the way that will resonate with you.

2. Go where the road leads you. The checklist will only wear you out.
3. Be true to yourself. Figure out exactly what is right for you and do it. Chances are, if you're feeling stressed, you're living someone else's pilgrimage.
4. Meditate. Find a quiet place and draw a circle around yourself to designate sacred space. Sit or stand inside the circle and let your mind go quiet. Study the things causing stress as if from an outside perspective. When you decide to leave, step across the threshold of the circle and leave all your stress behind.

LONELINESS

If you travel alone (and sometimes even if you travel with others), loneliness, I believe, is the greatest challenge of all on a pilgrimage. Here is the best way I've found to not only deal with but to turn this difficult trial into the most powerful of internal transformations.

1. Simply throw yourself into humanity. Don't reach out with desperation; rather, embrace everyone around you with openness. Don't be afraid; be open.
2. Once you're open, once your energy is clear, and you're at peace with being by yourself, you'll suddenly have all the friends and companions you could ever ask for. By first overcoming the need for companionship, you will naturally draw other people to you.
3. Stay true to what you wanted out of the journey. Keep focused on your shrine or your objectives (like visiting the world's great baths) and make as few plans as possible. Open up to the beautiful serendipity of the pilgrimage, and you'll awake one day and realize with quiet amazement: *I haven't felt alone for a very long time*.

REACHING THE END OF THE ROAD

Sometimes on a pilgrimage you literally reach the end of the road. In these moments when the initial reason for the journey seems to be

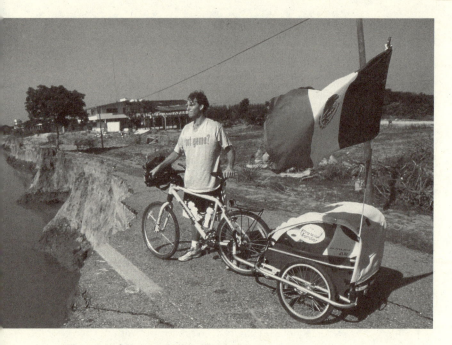

The end of the road (literally) in Mexico

completely irrelevant and you honestly wonder why in the world you're there, trust that perhaps there is a deeper purpose to the journey than you could have originally envisioned and that the new purpose, your **new road**, is about to be revealed as long as you continue.

BRINGING BACK YOUR HEART

You may face loneliness, sadness, fear, loss, heartbreak, anxiety, monotony, or desperation on the pilgrimage; you may long to turn around, go home, and abandon the quest. Under such circumstances it is common for pilgrims to exert their energies of hope and desire in a thousand different directions, seeking some sort of relief. Ultimately, though, this just leads to exhaustion and accomplishes little. The pain must be dealt with from within. I call this bringing back your heart. Here is how to start.

1. Find a peaceful place where you can think, like a glen, a park, a sugarcane field, or a waterfall.
2. Imagine all the hopes, desires, and needs flying out of you in a million different directions. Gather up these energies and return them to you.
3. Focus all this energy on inner peace instead of an outward means of solving the problem. Let your heart return to you.
4. Ask yourself what it is you really need. Is it companionship, guidance, a good *sopa de mariscos*? Hone in on the essential thing you feel is missing. Sometimes, we get so wrapped up in the feelings the problem gives us, we are unable to articulate the things we need to help us move forward past the situation.
5. When you feel you have reached an answer to that question and found that peaceful place within, your heart has returned to you. Leave the forest, glen, sugarcane field, or wherever and continue the journey. Calmly and patiently look for the things you need. No doubt they will come to you now.

My sister Alicia has been in Paraguay for a year. She's a Peace Corps volunteer, holed away in her tiny "clubhouse bungalow" (the term I use for her one-room shack) deep, deep in the campo. She's a five-mile walk followed by a dusty, bumpy, hour-long bus ride from the nearest town with ice cream.

The backpacks are packed, the tears cried, the clubhouse bungalow empty, but it isn't time for her to go. It has only been a year and volunteers agree to stay for two. But she is at the end of her rope and asks me in a letter what I think she should do.

I read her letter from a hotel in West Yellowstone, Montana, where I'm a desk clerk trying to figure out what to do next with my life. I write back and tell her to **bring back her heart.** She sits on a stump in the front yard of the bungalow, surrounded by farms and forests and people she still doesn't quite understand, reads the letter, focuses on calming all her loneliness and fear and on bringing back her heart. And her next year in Paraguay is one of the best of her life, which leads me to a parable . . .

THE PARABLE OF THE HEART

Frustrated with life and recently rejected by one of the best kissers I have ever dated (a week before Valentine's Day, no less), I reached a rather low point. And it was at that moment that I saw a bowl of valentine hearts on the table in my apartment. As I passed that bowl, I swore to the universe that I would live by whatever mantra I drew from the valentine hearts.

I dug through the bowl without looking and picked out a heart. Outside, I opened up my hand and looked at it. And it said:

be true.

It didn't say: *one kiss* or *loverboy* or something silly like that. It said *be true,* the most important thing a pilgrim can do. I ate the heart as a sacrament to this all-important mantra and have not forgotten it since.

Pilgrim's Prayer
May you believe
Whomever you seek
you are

Whatever you need
you have

Wherever you go
is home

                    —*Yvonne Lynn*

CHAPTER 9

The Magic and Other Pilgrim Gifts

A JOURNEY FROM WEST TO EAST, TO BRING A MAN BACK TO LIFE

"In the summer of 2003, I packed up a minivan in San Jose, California, and headed east. My destination was Saint John's, Newfoundland, the oldest city in North America and the farthest point east on the continent. I was on a quest to capture and record memories. Seventeen months prior, my best friend had been killed and I decided immediately to make a documentary film about him, to collect every memory of his life from everyone who ever knew and loved him before those memories faded into the mists of time. In doing so, I met dozens of people and saw dozens of places that he had spoken of in our time together, but which I had only previously imagined. I saw our great country for the first time; visited places that were sacred to him; met his rich array of family, friends, and colleagues; and even stood at the spot where he died. But the true carrot of my journey awaited me in the east, where the land would finally run out.

"In the city of Saint John's, there lived a little boy, just shy of one year old. He was my friend's only son, born after his death, his last living remnant on this earth. He would never know his father, and it was for this boy that I was making this movie, so that through the immortal magic of motion pictures, they could one day meet. I shall never forget the moment when, after many weeks, thousands of miles, and memories, I finally reached a little basement apartment. In the living room, I was handed my friend's son. At first, he was scared of me and wouldn't face me. Finally, I gave him a big kiss, and he laughed and smiled right at me. He had his father's smile. And I felt once again that my friend lived."

—*Kurt Kuenne, filmmaker, Burbank, California*

Moon over volcanic field in Iceland

Since time immemorial, pilgrims have been imbued with special gifts when they embark on their journeys. As you get deeper into the quest, you will notice these gifts more and more. The process of refining yourself via the trials and miracles of the road makes the gifts of the pilgrimage more apparent. It is as if they were there all along, but it takes the clarifying process of a pilgrimage, with all its requisite *luz y sombra*, to really make them evident. Here are a few examples of these gifts.

THE MAGIC

The Magic flows through every pilgrim. It is the pilgrim's ability to work the little miracles along the road, like finding free stuff to eat, stumbling across the perfect campsite, meeting that life-changing road trip soul mate, or getting into places you would otherwise find impervious. If you wonder why you tend to meet more people on a pilgrimage, why everyone and everything feels more genuine, why things seem to flow more smoothly, it is because of the Magic.

As a road trip pilgrim, you already have the Magic. Here's how to feel it and use it.

1. Retain complete faith and confidence in pulling off the impossible, but be open to the impossible working out in unexpected ways.
2. Remember, you are a pilgrim. You are untouchable. The world has no hold upon you. You are free. You are lost to the road.
3. Lean back on the Magic and become one with the road. Return to the moment. Rid yourself of all fears and regrets; cultivate joy, calm, and ease.

In Los Angeles on my four-month, ten-thousand-mile, book-tour pilgrimage, I wanted to get into the Roxy (the famous club on Sunset Boulevard) to see if I could find this waitress I'd met there a year and a half ago. I always wondered if I should have pursued her, and now was my chance to put it to rest. But the cover was thirty bucks, way beyond my pilgrim budget, and it was sold out anyway. Still, I had to get in.

My friend Kurt, who drove me down, asked me how this was going to happen. I said I didn't know but told him to swing back in fifteen minutes. "What if you don't get in?" he asked. "I'll get in," I said. So I went up to the door and walked right in. Evidently, the doormen were trading positions and I just so happened to arrive at the exact right moment. Ten seconds later or earlier and I would have had a problem.

After fifteen minutes of looking around, I actually found the girl, but remembered right off the bat why I hadn't pursued her in the first place. The Magic will assist you even if the outcome is not what you'd hoped for.

THE GIFT OF PERSPECTIVE

The gift of perspective is the pilgrim's ability to see the world from the twilight. On a pilgrimage you are both connected to the world and apart from it. The gift of perspective helps you get a grasp of your own life's trajectory and plugs you into everything around you. This perspective is rare outside the scope of the journey.

The gift of perspective has fallen upon me on many pilgrimages: one time, sitting on a rock by the Mediterranean Sea while walking from Cannes to Antibes; another time, thinking in a sugarcane field deep, deep in a campo in Paraguay; and a third time, waiting out the rain beneath the gigantic statue of Jesus at Corcovado in Rio de Janeiro, Brazil. Though worlds apart, all three moments were marked by a serene sense of mental and spiritual flight.

Memories come rushing in, especially old ones you haven't accessed for years. Emotions rush in, especially feelings of closeness with other people, even people you may not have spoken with in a long time, even acquaintances. In such moments you realize how interconnected we really are and how our impact on everyone around us cannot be underestimated.

PILGRIM'S NIRVANA

Pilgrim's Nirvana is the magical state that happens when the pilgrim is *lost to the road*. It comes upon you unexpectedly. You'll be ambling along when suddenly you realize that the world has no hold upon you. You are lost, free. It is a glorious feeling of liberation and rebirth, an emancipation from social constructs. Sometimes it comes and goes during a pilgrimage; sometimes it happens only once. There seems to be something about pilgrimaging in Latin America that evokes Pilgrim's Nirvana for me like nowhere else. Pilgrim's Nirvana can happen anytime, even when you're not on a pilgrimage.

GREAT MOMENTS OF PILGRIM'S NIRVANA

Highway 1, Maine, 3:10 AM. Clint and I are ambling down the road on an all-night hitchhiking extravaganza. Despite the fact that we haven't seen a car for a while, it's illegal to hitchhike in Maine after dark, Clint has a terrible toothache, and we have a hundred miles to go to get to Boston by 7:00 AM for an early flight, Pilgrim's Nirvana carries us away in the joy of the journey (and we ended up catching our flight).

Iguazú Falls, Argentina, 8:31 PM. Spray rising all around me from the great falls, I am rushed away in a surreal sense of timelessness and calm.

Ipiquari, Paraguay, 8:45 PM. It happened at a fruit stand at dusk, perusing gigantic bunches of globe grapes. My sister and I are gallivanting through the hinterlands of Paraguay; we've just hiked down from a church where we watched the sunset. Happy and at ease, we step over to the stand in the delicate evening dim, and suddenly, we're lost to the world.

Queens, New York, 6:23 AM. I awake in the tiny attic bedroom of my girlfriend Karien, a Puerto Rican immigrant and absolute sweetheart. "Do you want to see my park?" she asks. Down a forested lane in the morning light with broken glass glittering, we walk slower than I have walked in years, hand in hand, no rush, no hurry, and I am gone, gone, gone.

From this hour I ordain myself loos'd of limits and
imaginary lines,
Going where I list, my own master total and absolute,
Listening to others, considering well what they say,
Pausing, searching, receiving, contemplating,
Gently, but with undeniable will, divesting myself of the holds
that would hold me.
I inhale great draughts of space,
The east and the west are mine, and the north and
the south are mine.
— Walt Whitman (another nice passage
from Song of the Open Road*)*

MAGICAL REALISM

To see the world as it appears to be, but then to unveil its hidden layers, this is the essence of magical realism. *Magical realism* is a term often applied to art and literature where magic occurs in seemingly mundane settings. It's similar for the road trip pilgrim; it's just that the world is your canvas, your journey is your painting or your book, and you're composing it all as you go along.

A pilgrimage encourages the pursuit and attainment of magical realism like no other act, because the usual stresses, mundane nuisances, and lesser/greater social equations of life are stripped away. Under such circumstances, and with such openness, you really don't have to do much; just open yourself up to experience. The world will rush in and transform you forever.

Pilgrims who attain and practice magical realism never see the world the same way again, even upon their return. It is a sort of enlightenment, a rushing in of color and vibrancy, an increase in spiritual acuity.

MAGICAL PLACES ALONG THE WAY

There are magical places all around us. En route to your shrine, take every detour possible to a magical place. It will only enhance the journey. Don't fall victim to a checklist or tight schedule that may discourage spontaneous and uplifting trail spurs.

WATERFALLS

While on a pilgrimage visiting my sister in Paraguay, she took me on a hike through the sugarcane fields to a magnificent waterfall: Salto Cristal. Amazingly, few go there (save intrepid Peace Corps volunteers). It sits out in the middle of the campo, completely undeveloped, a hidden

Salto Cristal Falls in Paraguay

Waterfall in Iceland

jewel. My sister and I were never closer than during those hours spent soaking in the pool below the falls. When a pilgrim finds himself in such a spectacular natural temple, the whole journey becomes clear as his loves and friendships become stronger and purer.

Biking down the west coast of Scotland, my brothers and I stumbled across the Falls of Falloch. While not as pristine as its South American cousin, the falls had the same effect on us, though the midges were awful. Giant falls, such as Mosi-oa-Tunya (Victoria Falls) on the Zambia/Zimbabwe border, have tremendous, centering energy as well.

HOT SPRINGS

Clint honestly thought Zim's hot springs in Idaho would heal his pesky skin lesions. It didn't heal the lesions, but it put us in a terrific mood for the rest of the journey. Spiritually, hot springs have great power, as Jared and I discovered while backpacking to Angel Spring in the Yellowstone back-country. We pilgrim-baptized ourselves in the water, determined to set our gaze forward and shrug off regret. And I won't soon forget the evening I spent soaking with a bunch of Icelandic fisherman in their hometown hot spring overlooking a fjord in the isolated northern village of Talknafjurder.

Hot springs bring a pilgrim back to a sense of the present moment, the now. They can be a powerful force in aligning the pilgrim spiritually for the rest of the journey. And they're just darn fun.

HEALING SHRINES

My mom and I traveled through Costa Rica when I was a kid. We entered La Basílica de Nuestra Señora de Los Ángeles, Costa Rica's most famous shrine. My mom was limping so badly from a bout of arthritis she could barely walk. Inside, one touch of the sacred stone to her hip and the pain was gone. Our guide watched in amazement as she strode out of the shrine with no pain and no limp whatsoever.

Healing shrines are scattered throughout the world. Most have come into existence because they mark the site of a purported miracle or miraculous vision. They're interesting to visit as cultural icons and centers of faith and pilgrimage, and you may experience a miracle, too.

TEMPLES, STUPAS, AND OTHER HOLY PLACES

Approach the temple, stupa, or shrine with respect for the tradition, which may not be your own, and bring to it your own enthusiasm for what it represents. Make it personal and the temple will become magical to you, too.

MENHIRS AND STONE CIRCLES

On a healing pilgrimage through France, my uncle and I visited the ancient rock circles of Carnac on the northwest coast. People throughout history have found that such gigantic standing stones, or menhirs, have certain powers. Fertility rites, purification rituals, and, for us, pilgrimages often revolve around these great stones. Thousands of menhirs line fields in places like Carnac and Almendros in Spain.

TURNING THE EVERYDAY INTO THE MAGICAL

Any place can be magical, especially for a pilgrim, because the pilgrim carries **the Magic** with him wherever he goes. Use magical realism to transform any place or journey into something much deeper and richer.

To put the power of magical realism to work, you need to:

1. Cross the threshold into the place. The threshold can be any boundary, real or imagined.
2. Leave the world behind on the other side of the threshold. You are now on hallowed ground.
3. Imagine that time does not exist here. You can stay as long as you want. All you have is the moment, which is all we ever have anyway.
4. Commit to staying until you've found the peace you want.
5. Step back over the threshold into the real world and take the peace and the Magic with you.

A few everyday places turned magical:

THE UNIVERSE STONE AT THE COVE, NEW YORK CITY

Sure, it looks just like some big ol' cement-chunk remnant of whatever used to squat on this nice park on the Hudson River, but when I climb up on this stone and lie down, it becomes a shrine. The world ceases to exist and it's just me, relaxing back in the moment, absolving myself of any fear of the future, and letting the universe take over and guide me where it will.

THE TIME-FREE HAMMOCK, ANYWHERE, EARTH

Crawl into the hammock and it's much like the universe stone: time ceases to exist. String up the hammock in a dark room, jungle, forest, orchard, wherever. Float in the void and figure everything out. When you're ready to return to the real world, crawl out. Hammocks made by artisans work best as time-free hammocks. My two favorites are a handmade hammock from a village near Mérida, Mexico, and another from Asunción, Paraguay.

A SWIMMING HOLE, MOST PLACES, EARTH

In Haiti the street kids I worked with took me to a sewage-infested swimming hole. They were absolutely giddy, tearing off their clothes and diving into the water. This is where they go to bathe, to play, to relax. Most people would have seen a polluted stream; they saw a shrine.

You can make a magic place anywhere. Try simply drawing a circle on the ground and stepping inside. You have just designated magic space. Having such retreats on a pilgrimage is vital, providing a few moments for thought and repose. Here are a few more that have worked for us and can be found almost anywhere.

Open fields
Basketball courts
Mountaintops
Abandoned airstrips
Cemeteries
Forests and groves
Apple orchards

My rooftop becomes a magic place again and again.

Banana fields

Picnic tables

Sugarcane fields

Any place can become magical if you choose to make it so.

GOOD OMENS

If you're alert to everything going on around you during your pilgrimage, you'll come to realize that good omens are everywhere. These are the universe's way of encouraging and blessing the quest.

1. Biking into a rainbow. This omen foretells good luck, enjoyable riding, and the assurance of finding a five-star campsite at day's end.

2. Finding beauty in unlikely places. This omen heralds many magical moments of serendipity throughout the rest of the journey.
3. Coming upon a truck-going-downhill sign. This omen portends that you will soon be going downhill, possibly the best omen of all for the bike-bound pilgrim.

CHAPTER 10

Pilgrim Skills

LOOK UP!

"The dogwood willows and fallen trees were so thick I could hardly move forward another step, not that I knew where forward was anymore. The sound of the river was distant through the trees, but my sense of direction was gone and the brush was impenetrable. I couldn't tell a compass point in any direction. The late autumn sun was sinking fast. No matches, no tent, no food. I was a scared little pilgrim with sweaty palms. I gripped the worn wood stock of my .22 rifle. At least I could shoot something for supper or something that wanted me for supper if it came to that. When I was a little boy, my father told me there were bears down by the river. Now, lost and eleven years old, I had begun to wonder if he was serious. But I was glad to have the old Winchester with me.

"Then the revelation came. *Look up, look up!* Propping the rifle against a vine-covered log, I climbed a maple tree and just as I was about to run out of branches, I could see above the brush maze in which I had been lost. The Little Bear River sparkled in the late afternoon sun as did the small lake it emptied into. The lake pointed the way home and I was there in a few hours.

"That experience has served me well over the decades as I've traveled to great places. It gave me the courage to find kind people on the gritty sidewalks of Manhattan; to call on Key West's stern undertaker and hear how it was for him growing up on the island; to befriend a Puerto Rican politician in Washington, DC, who told me his story of immigration, education, and ascendancy in government.

"It is from these journeys that little boys, who think they've grown up, come to appreciate the fragrance of the islands after a rain, the grip of a solid hand in a foreign land, and the realization that you will find your way home."
— *Mike Stauffer, retired deputy sheriff, Cache Valley, Utah*

A pilgrimage is a spiritual quest, and yet, to proceed, or at least to proceed in comfort, you must master certain skills. Some are practical, some are fun. First the practical . . .

SHELTERS, POLICE ESCORTS, AND FIXING STUFF

Your pilgrimage will teach you many things that will prove invaluable on the road. Once you're home, you're not going to be building rain shelters all the time, but when you're on the journey, such skills can mean the difference between a nice night reading and sipping hot chocolate while listening to the rain and an uncomfortable night crammed into a mildewy tent.

CONSTRUCTING A RAIN CANOPY

Rain shelters are a simple way to protect most campsites from the rain and enhance the journey by providing some meditative time at the end of the day to read, relax, write, or chat.

Basically, you need three things:

1. A tarp
2. Rope or twine
3. Trees

Scout out a good campsite with ample trees spaced not too far apart. Tie the tarp between the trees, angling it downward so the rain will drain off. You may also want to weigh down one corner with a bike lock to provide a more effective rain escape (if it's really pouring) or to balance the torque.

Classic Rain Canopy, Summit Lake, West Virginia

twine attached to trees

twine attached to trees

tarp

picnic table dry! →

hanging U-lock to balance torque

Classic Road Trip Pilgrim Shade Structure Near Star Valley, Wyoming

converted tent tarp →

bungee cord holding up log →

sun off happy pilgrims!

bike as anchor →

bungee cord anchored to tent stake

fallen log as anchor

stick holding up bike

CONSTRUCTING A SHADE STRUCTURE

Escape the sun beneath a shelter made from the same three components as the rain canopy. If you find an area with well-placed trees, then follow the same steps above. If there are no trees, try using bikes, tent poles, sticks, or other available means. It doesn't need to be big or high; you just want enough room for you and your fellow pilgrims to stretch out underneath during the hottest part of the day. And, if you run out of twine or rope, bungee cords have myriad uses. Give them a whirl.

GETTING A POLICE ESCORT

As I mentioned in the chapter on camping, cops may surprise you with their helpfulness. Like almost everyone else, they'll probably find your quest interesting and may want to pitch in.

On two occasions biking through Mexico, I was riding late and the cops actually approached *me*, concerned for my safety. On both occasions they escorted me to safe, secluded campsites. In New Jersey we got a police escort across the Outer Bridge onto Staten Island because, well, I guess we were convincing and we had **the Magic** working for us.

To get a police escort, go to a place where you can find a helpful cop: a convenience store, diner, or a block or so away from a police station. Simply explain to the cops why you need a police escort and use the Magic to gently convince them.

FIXING ALMOST ANYTHING WITH DUCT TAPE

Duct tape is the indispensable cure-all for the pilgrim, and fixing things with it is easy. Just make sure you have plenty of it and that it is a solid name-brand kind. Generic brands of duct tape don't work quite as well. Use a few of those pennies saved from caching ketchup packets to upgrade your duct tape.

A few examples of things we have fixed over the years with duct tape:

- **Broken bike frame.** Clint's bike busted a weld coming off Engineer Pass in Colorado. We taped it up tight and it held until we got to Denver, two hundred miles later.
- **Flat tire.** We were out of patches, but duct tape worked. Not well, but well enough to get us to the next town.
- **Broken pack frame**. I think duct tape is *still* holding that thing together.
- **Water-bottle leak, flesh wound, tourniquet (heaven forbid)** . . . You can fix almost anything temporarily with duct tape.

BASKING IN YOUR OWN GLORY AND SKIPPING ROCKS

Aptitude in the following areas won't save you from sunstroke or sleepless nights, but they are good skills to have for upping the fun quotient on your pilgrimage.

HOW TO GET IN SMALL-TOWN NEWSPAPERS

Out in the boondocks, small-town newspapers will go nuts for your quest, anything to liven up the news of Jim Mason's prize pumpkin, beer prices at the Quickie Mart, or how much rain has been measured so far this year. Here are surefire ways to get noticed.

1. Camp out in the town park and sleep in. This will make you more visible.

2. If you're desperate for attention, pop into the newspaper yourself. Chances are they'll run some sort of blurb about the journey just to get rid of you. (That poser pilgrim in Northern Ireland I mentioned earlier had a racket going by just showing up at newspapers and refusing to leave until they finally printed something about him. Not recommended.)

3. Befriend a well-connected local who will pitch your story to the paper.

We got in the paper after surviving a massive thunderstorm in Nebraska City, Nebraska. While hanging out in Ten Fountain Square in Cincinnati, Ohio, we were written up in the paper after being approached by two reporters on their lunch break. In Illinois a **curious local**, the town clown as it turned out, got us into the local paper. The curious-local technique also worked for us in Las Vegas, Nevada; in Springfield, Massachusetts; in Villahermosa, Mexico; and in many other places along the way. Nothing is quite so fascinating to stagnant folks as a road-tripping pilgrim.

MAKING A MOVIE ABOUT YOUR ADVENTURE

I've directed a full-blown documentary or smaller vignette about most of the pilgrimages I've taken. Whether a week-long jaunt around the ring road of Iceland, a three-week circuit of Cambodian temples and holy mountains, or a three-month mountain bike ride, making a film about your journey is one of the best ways to remember it, though it can make the journey more grueling too. Here are a few tips I've found helpful.

1. The trip and the film are one. We used to have endless philosophical debates as to which was more important, the trip or the film, because sometimes you shoot something and it disrupts the flow of the journey, while other times you shoot something and it enhances the journey. After all of this rumination and debate, we

concluded that there is no distinction between the trip and the film. Each is intricately linked to the other and an element of the overall experience.

2. Shoot everything from the "eye of the hurricane." You want to let the action take place all around you, not from a third-person perspective. This will draw the viewer into the film and keep everybody feeling like they're part of the action. The eye of the hurricane is a shooting style we developed on our 800-mile pilgrimage to Jack and Dan's Tavern in Spokane. It involves a psychological and creative shift: Instead of seeing the journey from an outside perspective, we envisioned it happening all around us and tried to capture and present it as such for the audience.

3. Take turns shooting so no one feels like the designated camera person. If you're traveling with fellow pilgrims, you want everyone to feel equal. Swapping the camera around helps maintain the eye-of-the-hurricane style as well.

4. Do exactly what feels right to you. The film is the inward journey; the trip is the outward journey. Each should be approached as a true pilgrimage, where you do exactly what you want. Don't let thoughts of potential marketability skew decisions. Keep both journeys pure.

5. Don't worry if you only have a basic camcorder to shoot the piece. Content is everything. The audience will forgive anything except for an uncompelling story.

SHOOTING WHILE RIDING YOUR BIKE

1. Relax and trust your bike and the road.
2. Practice riding without your hands first.
3. Get a mental read of the road before looking at the pop-out screen or viewfinder.
4. Develop a sense for where the camera is shooting without having to look in the viewfinder. Instinctive shooting is key.

My road trip documentary *True Fans* became my breakout project, winning the Banff Mountain Film Festival People's Choice Award and touring internationally. It inspired a musical by the same name from a Broadway producer and helped get my first book published, all because I made the film I wanted to make. Stay true to yourself, your craft, and your pilgrimage.

SKIPPING ROCKS LIKE A PRO

One of the great benefits of going on a pilgrimage is getting darn good at skipping rocks. Think athletic stance. Bend the knees. Think flick of the wrist. Think a sidearm pitch and a clean follow-through.

Micah's got a very masculine follow-through going on there (see photo); his pitch was worth at least a dozen skips. Jared's follow-through is nice and crisp. If the surface is still and the rock's round and smooth and dense, you can skip for miles.

CHAPTER 11
Seeking Wisdom and Falling in Love

A SOLO ODYSSEY AROUND LATITUDE ZERO
DOCUMENTING EQUATORIAL LIFE

"Octavio Paz so eloquently states that 'each poetic adventure is distinct and each poet has sown a different plant in the miraculous forest of speaking trees . . .' My circumnavigation around the equator was a quixotic quest, not seeking definitions but pure movement. I was following the patterns of the butterflies, the flight of the frigate birds, the trenches of the great bodies of water . . . fatigue too boring, conflict too outdated, and cynicism too apparent. I just decided to align my soul with the wind and go into the wilds,

© Monique Stauder

the villages, and the cities along latitude zero, appreciating the oneness of all, allowing ever-present light to shine through me. The creative result was poetic and raw, a unique documentation of the ebb and flow of humanity and nature around earth's great circle." *www.moniquestauder.com*
— *Monique Stauder, photojournalist,*
Bangkok, Thailand

© *Monique Stauder*

As road trip pilgrims, finding that nugget of wisdom that guides us for the rest of our lives or that magnesium-fire romance that we remember forever is at the heart of the quest.

THE WISDOM OF THE ROAD

The guru who blessed your journey was probably the first wise being you encountered, but he or she is by no means the last. Have a question? Need help controlling the weather or choosing your next path? While on a pilgrimage, wisdom is often as easily accessible as having a need or desire and projecting it out there.

DEALING WITH WITCH DOCTORS

Witch doctors use their knowledge of the occult and their special powers to make women fall for you or cause people to drop dead. There are
two main kinds of witch doctors (I am using the Latin American termi-
nology as these are the types I have had the most experience with):

White witch *(brujo blanco),* who derives his power from the light

Dark witch *(brujo negro),* who derives his power from the darkness

When in need of the services of a witch doctor, follow these simple
steps.

1. Ask locals for their recommendations of the best witch doctor for
   the job. Often, they will be happy to lead you to the witch doctor's
   lair and even give you advice for your visit. They may also be able
   to corroborate the witch doctor's authenticity and the potency of
   his magic.

2. Always tip the witch doctor. Usually they don't have an established
   fee; you just give them whatever you want. Don't be cheap, though.

I wanted to make it snow in the Yucatán Peninsula on New Year's
Eve at the end of my Mexico pilgrimage in December 1999. So I hunted
down a *brujo blanco* in Catemaco, Mexico, a lakeside town in the magical, hilly region near the Isthmus of Tehuantepec. Catemaco is famous
as a world center for witch doctors. They even have a conference there
once a year. Despite claims of having caused dozens of couples to fall
madly in love, making it snow in the Yucatán was just out of this *brujo
blanco*'s league.

So I went to find a *brujo negro.* A local guided me to his house, which
looked just as you'd expect: dark, dilapidated, off-kilter, like it had been
hit by a hurricane and had never recovered. It sat apart on a lonely block
as if all the other houses had gotten spooked and split. After meeting his
sallow henchman, I was admitted through a tiny door into a room where
graphic images of devils adorned the walls. And then the *brujo negro*
entered. He never sat down; he just stood over me, his eyes blazing like
he was just waiting to unleash the fires of hell upon me. Right off the bat
I figured that meteors falling from the sky might be a possibility with this

guy, but happy snowflakes? Probably not. And in my haste to get out of there, I forgot to tip him. A few days later I got deathly ill.

Always tip the witch doctor.

Most cultures have some sort of witch doctor variation, be it a shaman, a priest, a healer, or an oracle. In Haiti I visited a voodoo doctor in his Cite Soleil bungalow. He wasn't able to help me capture the affections of this beautiful relief worker I'd fallen for, but he did say he'd work on the snow thing.

IF YOU BREAK IT, HE WILL COME (FAITH IN THE FIXER GURU)

Just like the spiritual guru you will no doubt meet on your quest, the fixer guru is out there too. He or she is just waiting for the moment of your greatest need. When that moment comes, the fixer guru will appear. You must simply have faith and use **the Magic**.

The hitch on the Ark of the Covenant snapped. About the time I noticed this, and began to wonder what in the world we were going to do, we rolled into the little town of Parlin, Colorado. And here we met Chuck Glaze, a western romantic who could fix anything and had the tools to do it. He engineered a new carriage bolt for the Ark and we were rolling in no time.

Only minutes after severely bending a rim while heading up to Spokane, a fixer guru (and fellow biker) arrived on the scene. He was able to bang the rim back into shape with a tree branch.

When the Ark broke down in

Mexico, Randel and his wife, Araceli, came along and offered all the help I needed to continue the quest.

LOVE ON THE PILGRIMAGE

There's nothing better than a little romance on a pilgrimage. And in terms of gaining wisdom, nothing quite compares to meeting that road trip soul mate who just seems to get you like nobody ever has. The relationship may not last; it may be only for the now, but that's fine. Enjoy the moment and see where it goes.

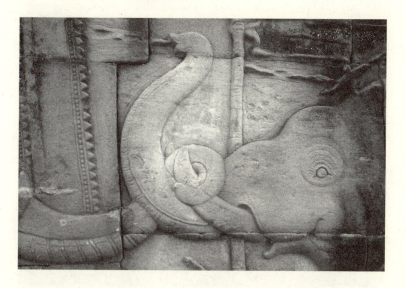

FINDING FLOWERS IN A DEVELOPING COUNTRY ON VALENTINE'S DAY

It is almost inevitable that you'll find yourself on a pilgrimage in a developing country on Valentine's Day with no clue how to find fresh flowers for a beautiful girl you just met.

From my own various experiences in this predicament, here's what you can do.

1. Employ a street kid or other knowledgeable street savant to take

you around. This has to be somebody who has ample time to pour into the quest. It may take a while. You must be diligent!

2. Explain to your savant the importance of finding fresh flowers and tell him you'll buy him something cool if he succeeds.

3. Go to the more affluent suburbs where fresh flowers are most likely to be found. You may also consider pillaging a public or private garden, raiding the Imperial Palace (make sure you have bribe money for the guards if caught), or taking a jaunt out into the countryside for wildflowers. Tourist or expat enclaves are also a good bet.

4. Search until you find the flowers. Remember, you must be diligent to succeed.

I met a beautiful relief worker in Haiti. It was Valentine's Day and I had to get her flowers. I told Junior, one of the street kids I was working with, that I'd buy him some new pants if he helped me find some *"fle fre."* Junior was in. I think he got the *"fle"* part right (that's flowers) but he didn't understand my accent when I said *"fre"* (fresh). An hour-long ride later in an overloaded *tap tap* (a pickup-truck taxi), we ended up in the central market where Junior pointed triumphantly to some nasty, plastic funeral flowers and told me to pay up.

"Fle_*fre!* Junior! Fle_*fre!*" Plastic flowers for Valentine's Day?! We ended up in Petionville, a more affluent suburb, where a temporary fresh-flower market had been set up in the town square. I put together a killer bouquet and even wrote her a poem.

FALLING HEAD OVER HEELS ON A PILGRIMAGE: A WORD OF CAUTION

Warning, my road trip pilgrim friends, when you're on a pilgrimage, your emotions are piqued! Falling head over heels in love is easier on a quest than it is back in normal life. Others sense your joie de vivre, and **the Magic** too, and are just naturally more drawn to you. Plus, when you're on a pilgrimage, there is no guarantee you'll ever see each other again, so giving it a whirl becomes less of a risk. That said, here are a few things to help you keep some sort of perspective when you feel yourself starting to fall.

1. Remember, you are a pilgrim. You are leaving town (tomorrow, Tuesday, next week). You must continue the quest!

2. When on a pilgrimage, everything is intensified. She suddenly seems like a goddess, which is good and may be true, but bear in mind that under such circumstances your chances of thinking and acting lucidly are somewhat impaired.

3. Calm down. You probably *have* felt this way before, even though you haven't.

4. Talk it over with your fellow pilgrims if you have any. They will help you make sense of the situation and provide you with some perspective.

5. Camp far from any sort of civilization. A communion with nature may help, or it may drive you crazy.

6. Pour all your emotions into your journal. This will also help you make sense of things.

What You DO Have (Remind Yourself of this Stuff)

a devil-may-care attitude

cachet—you're a pilgrim!

great muscle tone

a great tan!

MEETING AND IMPRESSING GIRLS WHILE HOMELESS, SWEATY, AND BROKE

This is not necessarily a guide to picking up chicks on a pilgrimage, because as a road trip pilgrim, you're seeking something deeper, even if it lasts only a day or a weekend. The romance found on the road is spiritual, it's emotional, it's . . . well, OK, it's blow-your-mind physical too, but you get the point. Anyway, with deference to my female pilgrim readers, here are a few things to remember to enhance your pilgrim mojo and hook up for a passionate, transcendent romance during the quest.

1. The trick is playing to your strengths: vagabondery. The fact you have said to hell with society and paychecks and stability and you're out on the open road, soaking up life, can be very attractive, depending on the girl.

2. Equally important is remembering why you chose to go on the pilgrimage in the first place. This isn't a spring-break keg-a-thon;

this is a pilgrimage with a distinctive, personal spiritual component. You aren't after physical gratification per se; you're after something deeper.

The girl who falls for the pilgrim falls for the mystique of the pilgrim. She doesn't care that you're eating peanut butter sandwiches four times a day! A massage therapist in Ouray, Colorado, saw us biking through town and wasted no time inviting us over for a day's-end rubdown. Too bad she was creepy.

Beautiful Sarah approached us on the steps of the Lincoln Memorial and invited us over for the night, sweat and all.

And on my book-tour pilgrimage, I met Erin, who encouraged me with a smile as I read at the Greenwich Village Barnes and Noble, and two months and many emails later, we got together. I'm still in touch with several girls I've met during pilgrimages over the years, and I remain grateful to each of them for edifying the journey and my life.

What You DON'T Have (Don't Think About this Stuff)

1. money
2. a home
3. a bed
4. a dog
5. a job

HOW TO WRITE A ROMANTIC POEM

Flowers are good. Poems are good, too. But it's like Stephen King says, you can either write, or you can't. If you can't write and you're determined to send her a poem anyway, this is what you do.

1. Find a really cool one that someone else has written already. Tear it out of some old poetry book you may find in a used bookstore along the way.
2. Or, you can try to write your own. But beware, your emotions are heightened. You may look back and realize it was a bad idea. If you do decide to write your own, make it short, vague, and esoteric. She might actually think it's brilliant. Maybe it is brilliant.

As if finding flowers for that girl in Haiti on Valentine's Day wasn't enough, I concluded that I should write her a poem, too. It was darn good, one of my best. I read it to her on the roof of her house in Port-au-Prince after giving her the flowers. She sorta sat there for a moment before saying: "You're a pretty good writer." That was it.

Like I said, when you're on a pilgrimage, your emotions are enhanced and you may not be thinking clearly.

EMPLOYING A WITCH DOCTOR TO COMPEL HER TO FALL IN LOVE WITH YOU

All else has failed: the charm, the flowers, the poems. You're totally in love and she won't give you the time of day. Now it's time to pull out the big guns.

1. Find a nice **brujo blanco.** This kind of witch doctor specializes in love. Ask around; the locals will know where to find him.
2. Ask to see his list of clientele. Usually the *brujo* will post photos on his wall of all the happy couples he's helped. If the brujo has no "references," as it were, move on.
3. Peruse the photos and make sure the people are for real. Look for genuine signs of being in love. Nothing too obvious: the subtle touches, like that little twinkle or the way they hold hands. Don't be fooled by the poser *brujo*!

4. You need to tell the witch doctor how amazing the girl is and how great you will be together. You will also probably need to show him a picture of her.
5. Most witch doctors work off a donation schedule. You decide how much to give. Give him a decent amount, though. An angry *brujo* will only serve to staunch the Magic; you want the witch doctor firmly in your court.

DEALING WITH A LONG-DISTANCE ROMANCE WHILE ON A PILGRIMAGE

If you already have love in your life and you decide to leave her behind for a bit and go on a road trip pilgrimage, here are a few things to keep in mind to retain your sanity during those long weeks away.

1. Write her letters instead of making phone calls. Cheaper and more romantic anyway, it also helps maintain some psychological distance, which can actually be good. Plus, she'll love getting postcards from all the cool places you're passing through.
2. Collect a vial of sand/water at journey's end to give to her when you return. Little tokens like this make great, thoughtful gifts.

Disclaimer: OK, I have to be honest. This is the advice I wrote *before* a recent pilgrimage to Southeast Asia. You always think you're so tough until True Love knocks the wind out of you. You see, I met beautiful Heike only a few weeks before I left on the trip and was utterly smitten. Seemed like such brutal irony to meet the woman of your dreams before embarking on a long pilgrimage! Anyway, radio silence and the "romance" of writing postcards and collecting vials of water for a month was just not going to cut it. *To hell with that crap! This is love, baby!* This is how I survived.

1. Bring your laptop or buy one before the journey and download Skype. For those of you who don't know what Skype is, it very probably saved my sanity (and my bank account) during that trip. Skype is a free software download. With Skype you can chat as if on the phone from computer to computer for free. If you call her cell or landline from your laptop and she lives in the United States or Canada, no matter where you're calling her from, you can buy a yearly plan for pennies and call all you want. Otherwise, the rates of Skype to phone are reasonable.

2. Check into guesthouses with reliable Wi-Fi. If the Wi-Fi is free, you can chat for hours on your laptop for nothing. I spent many a night roaming the courtyard of the Villa in Siem Reap, Cambodia, with my laptop microphone pressed to my face, much to the amusement of the Khmer staff (one fellow declared in wonder that I had "the best laptop ever"). Skyping from the friendly confines of your guesthouse beats the heck out of that smelly Internet café on the corner, and you'll more than make up for the extra money spent versus a cheaper room in money saved. (I estimate my girlfriend and I Skyped for an average of three to six hours a day for eighteen days. Let's just say that comes to around ninety hours, a conservative estimate. Ninety hours at the Internet café at twenty-three cents a minute will end up costing you $1,242.00! Don't think you can afford that new laptop? Guess what, you just bought it with calling fees.)

3. Long online chats via gmail are also quite fun and help develop the relationship in different ways.

Now, I know you pilgrim purists out there are bemoaning this advice, and before that Southeast Asia trip I might have agreed with you. But when you get right down to it, the pilgrimage of True Love is the greatest journey of all. Don't let it get away.

CHAPTER 12

Arrival at the Shrine and the Journey Home

THE GREATEST JOY

"There was a period in my life where I worked for over three years without taking a vacation. This wasn't by design; it was just bad planning on my part. Now, I really enjoy summers and, since I missed three summer vacations in a row, I decided I was ready for a great one.

"The same single-mindedness of purpose that drove me to work three years without a vacation now drove me to put all efforts into planning the ultimate summer vacation. I was going to go on a pilgrimage to enjoy summer for eight months. I would start in the Southern Hemisphere in their summer and work my way north as I traveled around the world.

"On my travels, I snorkeled in the warm waters of Tahiti. I parasailed around an island in Fiji. In New Zealand I rafted off a twenty-one-foot waterfall and through an underground river; I swam with dolphins and bungee-jumped off a 300-foot bridge. I learned how to scuba dive on the Great Barrier Reef.

I bribed police officers in Bali who had made up charges and threatened to put me in jail. I traveled rivers in Thailand on small, handmade bamboo rafts. I climbed on the Great Wall of China. I played basketball on a dirt court in the Mongolian steppes. I took the Trans-Siberian train from Beijing to Moscow. I rode elephants, camels, and yaks. I panned for gold, dug coal, and climbed glaciers. I sheared sheep, caught crocodiles, and milked rattlesnakes. I didn't wear long pants for eight months.

"As I traveled, I realized more and more that what truly mattered to me was the love and companionship of my daughter, my family, and my friends. I missed them and could not wait to get back to them. I learned that balance is a good thing. I learned to take time off to recharge my batteries regularly. But most of all, I learned that being around the people you love is the greatest joy of all."

> — *Leif Langensand, CFO for a venture capital*
> *fund and Vice Chair of Peninsula Habitat for*
> *Humanity, Palo Alto, California*

After many long, wonderful years, months, weeks, days, or hours, you have arrived at your shrine. As you approach it, relive the whole adventure in your mind. Every pilgrim's experience will be different, but here's what you might expect:

THE SHRINE

It may feel a bit anticlimactic arriving at the shrine. This is fine and actually good in a way, as it is a testament to the richness of the journey. You may find that the real moment of communion and completion comes not when you end the journey, but at unexpected places beforehand.

Going across America, Clint experienced a moment of elation and accomplishment when we hit the Atlantic Ocean in New Jersey, not when we finally made it to Springfield, Massachusetts, and the Basketball Hall of Fame. In Mexico my moment of elation came when I rolled into el Gran Hotel in Mérida after a miracle ride, still a day away from Chichén Itzá, the actual shrine. Sometimes the shrine is just an endnote. Don't expect more from it than it can give. Maybe it's just a place and it's anticlimactic and that's fine. It often works that way on a pilgrimage.

SO NOW WHAT?

Whatever feelings are going through you, here you are standing before your shrine, the object of your quest. So what to do now?

1. Take your time going home. Relish the end of the journey. Hang out. Relax. You worked hard to get here; don't just go rushing off.
2. Spend a couple days in the area. Decompress from the journey. Review the journey in your mind.
3. Have a celebratory feast. You have earned it. Always have a little extra cash on hand for a real meal at journey's end. Or use the Magic and get it for free.
4. Return home slowly. If you go home too quickly, some of the Magic of the pilgrimage may not have time to completely settle in.

Journey's end for our ride across America, the Basketball Hall of Fame

THE JOURNEY HOME

After returning home, you may discover that you have a few things to do. This is my to-do list after my Scotland pilgrimage. No matter how much you have to do, take some time to ease back into things, lest **the Magic** be lost too quickly. As soon as you get back, see that person you've been wanting to see all trip and reconnect with your friends at home.

TREATING POST-TRIP SYNDROME

Be aware that you may contract a case of PTS, or Post-Trip Syndrome. This refers to the natural letdown that often occurs after a journey, especially one that really transforms you. You'll ride a high for a few days, then suddenly, unexpectedly, hit the skids. Don't worry about it. It happens. And it will pass.

compile Power Books / 1200 1000 2000 4000 → Worldwide MasterCard

pay as you go 4 ft 4 memory / 4200 Amex Express Ryan

30 Jan 33

TRUTH is what you truly want.

2249

MONDAY:

No man
known to

1. Deposit 1500. — Clint - 222.8000 - 390.7926
   - TATTI - Cliff -
2. Cash Checks
3. Firm a Fee W. Stuf Sec.   David Ewell = 44. 561.4975
4. Meet w U6   Monte Bono - 4 @ 463-9022
   1. Chris's Site, mailkey
5. Diary, schedule shoot - travel   Elwood Norwalk
6. List of ALL debts   100 to P.O.
7. Call Larry - Sprinkler Systems
8. E-Mail Mel / All E-Mail —   Mail
9. Talk to Chir - Lise   G. Telefol
10. Follow-up LATEN RIGHTS Chris B.
11. CLEAN Thoroughly

1st Thing
12. Buy Bread, PB & J, Carrots, OJ, Eggs, butter, cheese, water,
13. Routine
14. Send off Camera (Can MAC, etc. - List of Problems.
15. Track Down Clint
16. Copy CD @ DSW
17. Send CD to Hudson Valley - Mail Now
18. Meet w LeTA
19. TB ~ GH
    1 More Tapes, Dishwash, deal to ship
20. Call Dan Rogers
21. Pay @ Base Camp
22. Follow-up - V. Williams rights
23. Type in Final Paper Cuts —
24. Call Airline —
25. New N.B.
26. Check 860. = from Asan for Tracey
27. Find Polartec Grant Thing
28. Apply for New FR First Mount w Body
29. See Lynn - Up?
30. Delete e-mails   Tampico
31. Dub for Hana Greening 32. Talk to Dan R.

Call up everyone you know, everyone you haven't seen for a while. Get together for lunch, drinks, and all-night chats. Toss yourself back into your social scene. The pilgrimage was all about you; now it's time to share.

HOW TO WIN BACK THE GIRL YOU LOST

Once again, the advice here is a bit skewed by my male perspective, but female pilgrims, please bear with me and extrapolate accordingly for your own experiences.

She broke up with you while you were gone but now you're home, empowered from the journey, breathing fire for life, and you want her back.

First, **what you might *think* you should do:**

1. Set up an evening to get together and chat. Don't be weepy and pathetic; be empowered! You just got off a pilgrimage!
2. Talk about the journey. Describe how it changed your life, your new life plans, all the amazing things you're going to do, like curing malaria and solving world hunger.
3. Show her carefully selected pictures of the quest. Photos that highlight your great tan and exemplary muscle tone. Remember the summit-flex pictures? Show these.
4. Tell her you're going to be so busy from here on out. The pilgrimage has made you ravenous for life and "there is so much good to be done."

And now, **what you really *should* do:**

Get together sometime and talk about *her*. She'll ask about the journey and you'll gladly share, but you've had a lot of time to focus on yourself over the last few months; see what *she's* up to and use your amplified appreciation of life and everything around you to truly engage with her. Sure, bring along some photos and things, especially the summit-sign flex shots, but mostly, just forget about the trip and yourself and focus squarely on her.

HOW TO LOSE THE GIRL YOU WON BACK

Upon your return from the journey, everything will look different to you, including your relationships. If your love is true and destined to last, the pilgrimage will have only made her more beautiful to you and you will enjoy an even deeper bond. However, if you realize that you're no longer right for each other, consider the following steps:

1. Talk about how you're going to go on lots of pilgrimages now and you're not going to be able to see much of her anymore.
2. Tell her how you feel this spiritual call to throw yourself recklessly into the gears of life and that you don't know how committed you can be to anything but the quest from here on out.
3. Tell her that you have become addicted to peanut butter sandwiches and you really don't want to eat anything else.
4. Tell her you are getting rid of your bed and all your earthly possessions, donating all your money to charity, and planning to live off the "kindness of humanity" for the rest of your life.
5. Tell her how overrated a home, a roof, warm meals, money, credit cards, and motorized transportation really is.

That should about do it. If she sticks with you after hearing all of that, you know she's either totally desperate or absolutely the one.

HOW TO FIND THE GIRL YOU WERE HOPING TO FIND ON THE JOURNEY BUT DIDN'T

There's no one to get back together with, no one to break up with. Instead you want to find that person you were looking for before and during the pilgrimage. Remember, you still have **the Magic** and you are now a transformed soul. This is hugely powerful and attractive to your as-yet-unfound soul mate. Your job is to hold onto the Magic and allow it to work for you.

Remember to:

1. Treat every day like you're still on the adventure.
2. Let the thrill of being on the road and the Magic of the journey animate everything. Make a run down to the park a pilgrimage,

cook up road trip fare on your camp stove for fun. Take bike rides around the neighborhood and imagine you're in Europe or Asia or high in the Sierras.

3. The inestimable *joie de vivre* the pilgrimage gives a pilgrim is the most attractive thing you have. People are attracted to joy. Endow every day with meaning and adventure.

As Indian mystic Ramana Maharshi famously said, "Wanting to re-form the world without discovering one's true self is like trying to cover the world with leather to avoid the pain of walking on stones and thorns. It is much simpler to wear shoes."

You have essentially done the same thing by going on a pilgrimage. Instead of physically remodeling the world, you've transformed yourself. This is the great blessing of the journey.

THE NEXT ADVENTURE

It will come. Be open to it.

> *He who binds to himself a joy,*
> *does the winged life destroy.*
> *But he who kisses the joy as it flies,*
> *lives in eternity's sunrise.*
> —*William Blake*

Epilogue

A PILGRIM'S PARABLE, PART II

Three weeks after two kids on a bike taught me the greatest lesson of the journey, my Mexico pilgrimage was in shambles.

Here's the scene: It's Christmas. I'm sicker than I have ever been, holed up in a room in Campeche, Mexico. On Christmas Eve, the Ark of the Covenant (my bike trailer) had broken down, this time for good. I gave the Ark and everything I couldn't carry on my bike, including forty hours of footage, to a couple of good Samaritans who said they'd send it all back to me and drove away.

Unfortunately, I also gave them my credit card and most of my cash.

I realized my mistake that night when I rolled into Champoton, a little coastal town. It had been the toughest ride of my life, fighting headwinds for hours through the darkest swamps and forests with little food or water. I went to midnight Mass and a family invited me over, but after dinner they told me there was no room for me to stay.

En route to a divey inn at 3:00 AM, I nearly got mugged; the next day, I rolled into Campeche and that's when I got sick.

My best friend had bailed on the journey mere weeks before the launch. The film I was making was a wreck; an offer from *National Geographic* was nixed; the girl I loved was back with her ex. Piece by piece,

I had lost everything of importance to me on the quest: from my map to my journal, to my bike trailer, to my friends.

Sometimes it happens like that on a pilgrimage.

So I lay there in bed for the third straight day wondering what to do, wondering how things could have gone so wrong.

When my friends and I go on pilgrimages, we live by the mantra of "whatever happens is best." Could everything that had happened in Mexico really be for the best?

That night, with everything at its worst, I decided that it must be. A few minutes later the illness passed. And in its place was a new feeling I hadn't felt in a long time.

You begin a pilgrimage with a vision of what you want to gain from the journey. What I'd wanted was a return of **the Magic** I'd felt strongly as a kid but only fleetingly since. We've talked a lot about the Magic in this book. At its deepest, it is a pristine connection with the world, a sense of identity, an innocence regained. And now, miraculously healed and utterly at peace, I felt all of that Magic again. It was as if it had never left.

Perhaps sometimes you have to lose everything to gain the one thing you truly want.

The next morning I rode 120 miles to Mérida before dinner. I had

never felt better. And the next day I ended the journey at the Great Ball Court of Chichén Itzá.

Reflecting below the ancient stone rings, I felt like the parable that began the pilgrimage had repeated itself at the end: The things that I thought would ruin me were, in fact, the things that saved me.

It often works like that on a pilgrimage.

. . . and by the way, the Ark of the Covenant is still lost somewhere in the Yucatán.

OATH OF THE ROAD TRIP PILGRIM

I _____ (the reader) am going to

_____ (ignore, remove, vanquish) anything that gets

in the way of taking that epic pilgrimage I've been meaning to

take to _____ (the Great Pyramids,

the Hagia Sophia, the home of my favorite microbrew, etc.).

I'm going to put aside _____ (menial job, the

dishes in the sink, that cappuccino addiction) for _____

(an afternoon, a week, a month, God only knows . . .) and

get going.

I'm not going to be discouraged by the ego-traveler; in

fact, my pilgrimage has never been done before, because

I am doing it. So, even though I may walk a path worn by

thousands (like El Camino), it will be a wholly unique and epic

quest. By turning the page, I take the Oath to make this thing

happen, to never compare, and to have the time of my life!

I _____ (the reader), take

the Oath and become . . .

The Road Trip Pilgrim.

DAN AUSTIN has explored old paths and new throughout the world. His directorial credits include *Petionville,* a documentary exploring the lives of Haitian street children, and *True Fans,* a documentary film about his three-month mountain bike pilgrimage across America. Since its release in 1999, *True Fans* has screened worldwide, inspiring a musical and a book by the same title, written by Austin. Austin is cofounder of the 88bikes project, which endows an orphanage in a different country every year with bicycles for all the kids as well as supplies and funds for upkeep and bike-repair apprenticeships. 88bikes has been featured on CNN and CNN International. A popular speaker on college campuses, Austin splits his time between New York City, the Wasatch Mountains of Utah, and the intimate and unique pockets of culture throughout the world. Visit his website at *www.roadtrippilgrim.com.*

Dan Austin with orphans at the Palm Tree Center in Phnom Penh, Cambodia

OTHER TITLES YOU MIGHT ENJOY

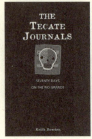

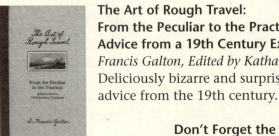